Newell Culver

Methodism forty years ago and now

Embracing many interesting reminiscences and incidents

Newell Culver

Methodism forty years ago and now
Embracing many interesting reminiscences and incidents

ISBN/EAN: 9783337259952

Printed in Europe, USA, Canada, Australia, Japan

Cover: Foto ©Andreas Hilbeck / pixelio.de

More available books at **www.hansebooks.com**

METHODISM

FORTY YEARS AGO AND NOW:

EMBRACING

𝕸𝖆𝖓𝖞 𝕴𝖓𝖙𝖊𝖗𝖊𝖘𝖙𝖎𝖓𝖌 𝕽𝖊𝖒𝖎𝖓𝖎𝖘𝖈𝖊𝖓𝖈𝖊𝖘 𝖆𝖓𝖉 𝕴𝖓𝖈𝖎𝖉𝖊𝖓𝖙𝖘.

ALSO,

THE RESPONSIBILITIES, PRESENT AND PROSPECTIVE, OF
THE METHODIST EPISCOPAL CHURCH.

By REV. NEWELL CULVER,
MEMBER OF THE NEW HAMPSHIRE CONFERENCE.

With an Introduction
By REV. LORENZO D. BARROWS, D.D.

Say not thou, What is the cause that the former days were better than these?
for thou dost not inquire wisely concerning this. ECCL. vii, 10.

———◆•◆———

NEW YORK:
NELSON & PHILLIPS.
CINCINNATI: HITCHCOCK & WALDEN.
1873.

PREFACE.

THE following pages were commenced without any intention of publishing a book. Being physically disqualified to perform further ministerial service among the people in person by reason of a long and severe sickness, the writer, for his *own* pleasure and profit, began to review the *social, numerical,* and *financial* condition of the Methodist Episcopal Church forty years ago—when he became one of her members—and to call to mind interesting reminiscences connected with his early ministry, and to compare *then* with *now.* He found increasing interest in the subject, and continuing to write, he at length, by the advice of valued friends, decided to prepare a book for the press.

He does not claim for it high literary merit. Historical or statistical errors may be found in it which have escaped the writer's notice; but he has the satisfaction of feeling that what he has recorded herein is in accordance with his best recollection of early Methodistic facts, with oral and written history, and recently published reports of our Church statistics and enterprises; and he hopes that the task thus performed, though imperfectly, which he finds to have been so agreeable and encouraging to himself, may be as pleasant and profitable to the reader.

THE AUTHOR.

INTRODUCTION.

THIS little volume is not the work of a croaker ;
no spirit of sour godliness runs through its
pages ; therefore it need not be read with any
allowance for unfounded prejudice or bigotry.
Though it is natural and common for those
who were active in years long gone by greatly
to magnify the excellences of the past and depreciate those of the present, this is not the
case with our author.

Nor is his work severely partisan or sectarian,
though it is thoroughly Christian, experimental,
and practical. It is not so much the object of
the author to disprove the doctrines and usages
of other Churches, nor even to defend those of
his own, as it is to set forth the particular operation of the Spirit in the awakening and conversion of men to Christ, and promoting revivals
of religion. It is therefore essentially a concise
and racy history of what God has wrought, and
how, for the last forty years, chiefly in the
Methodist Episcopal Church, beginning with

his own personal Christian experience, which is exceedingly pleasant and profitable to read. Whatever honors God and brings men to Christ seems to fill his soul with delight, and you read on and on, not wishing to pause.

We must never forget that those who have by long and successful experience reached the citadel of wisdom must not destroy the ladders by which they ascended, as the climbers after them, to the end of time, will need them. Progression is a series of stages. This book is a stage for the multitude, who can no more, at a single bound, reach the highest result of Christian and revival experience, than did the fathers, into whose labors we now enter. All must rise, if at all, by steps ; and as the great masses of the people are still engaged in the battle of physical and mental want, religious helps are as needful now as ever, or man's spiritual and highest nature will suffer loss, if not defeat, in the struggle. These helps are to come, so far as they are human, from the lessons of experience and history.

Herein lies the great excellence of this new book : it is a light now burning, which shines back over forty years, from which all lovers of

Christian experience see wrought out and worked over again what in substance they have experienced, strengthening and attaching them more and more to a vital religion. No pastor can read it and not feel quickened with renewed confidence in revivals and human efforts to promote them. It is good for all to live over again and again those rich and heavenly occasions of divine visitation when God has revealed himself in saving souls, founding and building up Churches. When the ministry, the Church, or individual Christians forget those revival occasions, they are drifting in other directions the Lord only knows where.

There is a strong tendency in all institutions and usages where human agencies are involved to this drifting spoken of, and if the agencies are chiefly human, that drifting is usually from good to bad, and from bad to worse. This is especially seen in all forms of human government, political institutions, and political parties. Nations, governments, and political parties, beginning usually comparatively in modesty, feebleness, and purity, grow corrupt as they grow old under their human manipulation, and they have crumbled to atoms, never to be exactly reproduced, with as much regularity and certainty as men march to the grave. They have survived longer or shorter, just in proportion as true and good principles have or have not been let alone by the poisonous hand of man.

But the Church is a divine institution, while the means for carrying it on are largely human ; hence there is danger to the Church that she may retrograde, her light grow dim, if not " become darkness," though her foundations of eternal truth cannot utterly or finally fail. This has often been the case ; but God, to prevent her overthrow, has always appeared just in her greatest emergency, and burst upon darkness and apparent destruction with some new light and means for her recovery and revival, wherein lies the difference between the Church and human governments and other earthly institutions. He has raised up men and measures unthought of, and often turned back the tide of death with a hand of power, though human, that has shaken the world.

The apostolic Church, commencing in strict spirituality and simplicity, soon grew powerful in numbers, then in wealth and worldly power ; then formality, pride, and worldliness followed,

till a dark night of a thousand years and Ro-
manism resulted. But God would not suffer his
Church to perish utterly, and so he raised up a
Huss, a Knox, a Luther, and others, to call it back
to first principles, and commit to the flames the
" senseless mummery " of mint, anise, and cum-
min, which had effectually excluded the weightier
matters of the law and the Gospel. Such is the
result of human hands tampering with Christ's
Church, putting into it what he has left out, and
leaving out what he has put in. The " inven-
tions sought out " by man to improve God's
work always mar it.

On a smaller scale the Church of England,
and indeed all other State Churches, continuing
a long time without interruption to work out
their legitimate fruits, show the historical fact
of a retrogression toward the " dark ages," and
a call for reformers such as Wesley, Whitefield,
Chalmers, and others like them, to save these
Churches from extinction. Reposing . upon
empty *forms* and a dead orthodoxy, they drifted
into the current with the world rather than
drew the world to Christ. Such a Church cannot be the Church of Christ—it *gathers* not
with him, but *scatters* abroad.

The history of the Puritans and the Pilgrims can hardly be regarded as an exception to this general fact in Church history. Much as there was that was good and apostolic in them, there was also something that must have been bad, as it has produced bad fruit in the shape of Unitarianism, Universalism, and "Liberal Christianity," or Infidelity. The *humanizing* hand has been too apparent in all these branches of the Church, hence they have suffered or been superseded by others, and so will it be with all others to the end of time which depart from the *spirituality* and *simplicity* of the Gospel.

The great practical and all-absorbing question with *us* is whether or not the career and history of the Methodist Episcopal Church shall be like or unlike those which have gone before it. Is *her* light also to become dim, her spirituality to depart, and her altars to be crushed with accumulating forms and empty ceremonies? Shall her numbers and wealth, and consequently her worldly power, lead her away into pride and abandonment of the meek and lowly Jesus? Why should we expect her history to be an exception to that of all other branches of the Church? Human nature and the world are

now as of old, and so is the philosophy of mind
and morals unchanged. The same humanity
enters into the modern as into the ancient
Church. And do not the signs of the coming
departure *already* begin to warn us ? A growing laxity in discipline, increasing devotion to
style and fashion, increasing members who
show no *heartfelt devotion to Christ*, hoarding
wealth while souls are perishing, and an infant
cry for "more ritual ;" the constant growth of
legislation in usages, forms, and machinery with
which we are loading the Church, thereby (necessarily) abstracting just that amount of attention from the vital and cardinal point—*spirituality*—all point in a direction of hateful memory, and should wake the attention of every
watchman on the walls of Zion.

Our hope that the future of our Church shall
be like its past all centers in this one thing,
namely, that she shall make the *spiritual* life of
God in the soul, the conversion of the world to
Christ, and the spread of scriptural holiness over
these lands *so cardinal and overshadowing* that
all our discussions and legislation on all side
issues and fixings shall be held comparatively as
mere dust in the balance. These are the days

of her greatest peril. Small numbers, feebleness, and persecution, have ever contributed to
spirituality and growth in the Church ; but
numbers, wealth, and power, to decline and
downfall.

Hence·this little timely book will be a most
valuable aid to our reading people, turning back
their minds to the days of our Church youth,
when she had nothing but her scriptural doctrines and usages to commend her to the public
favor, and thus grew with such unprecedented
rapidity. Nothing can reveal to us more clearly
than this whether or not the Church now is
advancing or retrograding in what renders her
really great and useful. This is the *vital* point
to be kept before the Church to aid her to with-
stand all the influences and temptations now
assailing her to let down her doctrines, usages,
and discipline. May the history of all Churches
instruct and warn us ! may the love we cherish
for the Church that, under God, sought and
saved us evermore, constrain us to hold fast to
her landmarks, and war valiantly against all her
insidious foes, and contend manfully for the
faith once delivered to the saints ! God forbid
that what he has given us by the high and holy

character and labors of our fathers should suffer in our hands, to the irreparable loss of those
who will come· after us ! Every age of the
Church has its responsibility. *This is ours*—
to " hold fast that which is good."

This line of thought will be strengthened if
we consult our own Christian experience. We
often find, when coldness and worldliness have
damped the fire of our Christian ardor and zeal,
doubts, fears, and, may be, skeptical thoughts
arise. Then, may be, we seek *arguments* to
re-assure ourselves. A Butler, a Paley, a Watson, a Whedon, reason with an irresistible force;
but nothing so quickly and effectually puts the
soul at rest, without one lingering doubt, as to
refer to our awakening and conversion by the
Spirit. In a moment the soul is filled with
assurance, and " we *know* whom we have believed ;" and " we know we have passed from
death unto life." The *power* of *Christian experience* in proof of the verity and divinity of
Christianity has no equal. Hence it was Paul's
sharp instrument in the most critical hour of
his eventful and brilliant life. It is a sad and
ominous day with the Christian when he forgets or thinks lightly of his conversion and con-

vert experience ; and as the Church is only the aggregate of individuals, it is equally sad for her when she forgets the days of her primitive spirituality and simplicity of purpose, with her holy zeal for Christ in the days of her "espousals."

As we have read this MS. book of modest pretensions, not so much for literary criticism and speculation as to refresh our mind with the early history, struggles, and achievements of our beloved Church, we have enjoyed much its happy, brief, and racy summary of her history, doctrines, discipline, and usages, set forth in no controversial but catholic and devout spirit ; and we have felt to thank God and the author for the soul-refreshment we have received from it, and really feel our piety quickened, and more intelligently, liberally, and devoutly attached to the Church than when we commenced it ; and we hope it may be so with the thousands who will read it. And may the beloved and afflicted author realize before he goes home to his final reward that, under God, he has done more for him and his Church in this unpretending publication than in all his previous life and labors !

L. D. BARROWS.

LAWRENCE, MASS., *Jan.* 1873.

CONTENTS.

CHAPTER V.

METHODISTIC CUSTOMS AND CHARACTERISTICS.

CHAPTER VI.

VISITING FROM HOUSE TO HOUSE.

CHAPTER VII.

CAMP-MEETINGS THEN AND NOW.

CHAPTER VIII.

PARSONAGES AND CHURCHES.

CHAPTER IX.

OPPOSITION TO METHODIST DOCTRINES AND USAGES FORTY
YEARS AGO, AND FRATERNAL RELATIONS WITH EVANGELICAL
CHURCHES NOW.

Contents.·   17

2

18   *Contents.*

CHAPTER XIV.

METHODISM AND THE ABOLITION OF SLAVERY.

CHAPTER XV.

LAY DELEGATION FORTY YEARS AGO AND NOW.

CHAPTER XVI.

NUMERICAL STRENGTH OF METHODISM FORTY YEARS AGO AND NOW.

Contents. 19

Contents.

METHODISM

FORTY YEARS AGO AND NOW.

Part First.

CHAPTER I.

My Early Religious Associations and Personal Experience.

THEN AND NOW.

FROM early life I have been somewhat familiar with Methodism. My father was a member of the first class formed on the "Old Barnard Circuit" in Vermont, in the early days of our Church in that State. In his days of active business life, he, for years, held official relations therein. My mother, though not a professor of religion, was deeply interested in the moral welfare of her household.

Our house was frequently favored with visits from many of those early veterans of the Cross, whose names are familiarly known in our Church histories. The influence they bequeathed to us is as fragrant as "the precious ointment poured forth." From a child I have heard their names spoken and their deeds praised. Many of these were our circuit preachers and frequent visitors at my early home. Their countenances, style of speech and dress, mode of traveling, manner of preaching, and general appearance, became familiar to me. Our house, being large, was sometimes opened, for the want of a more convenient place, for public religious services on the Sabbath and other days. These early associations had a powerful influence on my youthful heart and life.

When in my twenty-first year I sought, and I trust found, "the pearl of great price." I was then away from home, engaged in teaching. My denominational surroundings were very unlike those with which I had been previously associated.

The pastors of the different Churches were good men and popular preachers, and many of their members worthy Christians; but I could not be edified with the High-Churchism, and, to me, dull formalisms of the Episcopalians; nor with the Calvinistic and freely-expressed opinions concerning the fearful *danger* of entertaining a "false hope," held by the Congregationalists; neither with the sentiments, tenaciously advocated by the people called "Christians," with reference to the character of Christ, "the sleep of the dead," and "the annihilation of the wicked."

Though I sought to be faithful in Christian duties, and never failed to take some part in their social meetings, yet I found myself often unconsciously utteri ɔg sentiments which were adverse to theirs, sometimes subjecting me to the necessity of self-vindication.

Such surroundings and influences had an adverse effect upon my progress in the divine life. My experience was unsatisfactory. I could not tell the *time* nor *place* of my conversion, and had almost constant fears that I had not "passed from death unto life."

Well do I remember the first love-feast I ever attended, some months after I began the Christian life. The testimonies there given were very positively expressed. Various ones said that they *knew*, beyond the shadow of a doubt, that they loved God, and could tell just when and where they were converted. Such positive testimonies grated upon my ear. I thought they were a *little too certain* about it, and that becoming modesty required that they should be less positive.

After the love-feast was through my excellent pastor kindly asked me, "How did you like the meeting?" I answered, "Very well, only they were a *little too sure* they loved the Lord;" and believing him to be a judicious man, inquired, "Don't *you* think so too?" His reply disappointed me. It was this, "I am willing people should love the Lord, and if they *do*, it is proper that they should *say* so!" This was a kind and gentle rebuke to me for my uncharitable suggestion, and it had a good effect upon me. I concluded it was not best to complain of others for having reached an experience beyond my own. Though I could not say that I knew that I loved the Lord, yet, if others did, they might "*say so*," and I would try to love him too.

On the 15th day of July, 1832, I was baptized by our preacher in charge, Rev. E. Jordan, and received on probation into Society.

Having felt it to be my imperative duty to preach the Gospel, I began, with the approbation of my pastor, six weeks after this, my life-work, and continued to hold meetings to the end of my probation, when I was received into full membership in the Church, and at the same time was licensed to exhort. Three months after this the quarterly conference licensed me to preach, and recommended me as a suitable person to join the conference. The Rev. B. R. Hoyt, the presiding elder, immediately employed me for the remaining three months of the conference year to fill the place of the junior preacher, whose health had failed. Six months from the time of my reception into the Church I was admitted into the New Hampshire Conference, and received my first appointment.

My evidences of divine acceptance continued to increase, until at length I proclaimed to the people that " I too loved God with all my heart." Then followed "a great fight of affliction." " Satan desired to have me that he might sift me as wheat." Sift all the wheat out of me, and leave only the chaff. It was the hour of the "prince of darkness."

For the space of two weeks I remained in a state of deep despair. All hope of heaven had left me. I felt that I was surely doomed to eternal despair, and that already "the pains of hell had gotten hold upon me."

During all this time I did not question my duty to warn the people "to flee the wrath to come," as I visited from house to house, and kept on preaching according to previous notice. I even, conscientiously, refrained from speaking of my despairing feelings, lest I should wound

the precious cause of Christ. I could not
preach the *Gospel,* for this was *hid* from me, but
could and *did* "proclaim the day of vengeance ·
of our God." At length I found sweet relief
from this sad state of mind at a little old hut,
where lived a blessed saint of deep experience
in the things of Gospel grace, who was nearly
a hundred years old. By her godly counsel,
cheering assurances, and earnest prayers, light
dawned upon me, which gradually increased
unto a joyful, cloudless day.

Such a "horror of darkness" has never yet
returned to me. With my "shield of faith" I
have been enabled to "quench all the fiery
darts of the enemy." Indeed, when having the
"whole armor on, I have been conqueror, and
more than conqueror, through Him who has
loved me."

A sense of my unfaithfulness and weakness
has often oppressed me. I lament to-day that I
have not been, and am not now, a better Christian. But "I know whom I have believed, and
that he is able to keep that I have committed
unto him against that day" when he shall gather
his own into joys immortal. "The name of the
Lord is a strong tower ; the righteous runneth
into it and is safe."

This early experience I will now compare

with my present. In doing so I purposely omit to refer, with any definiteness, to my subsequent labors, conflicts, and triumphs while in the active ministry, as not relevant to my present arrangement of thought, and call the reader's attention to my more recent experience in the divine life. My fortieth year in the ministry began in utter physical prostration, great suffering, and almost certain prospect of death. I continued in this condition for about eight months, with no other expectation for the major part of that time than the daily prospect of exchanging earth for heaven.

During all this time I was sustained by the grace of God, comforted by the precious promises of his word, cheered by his conscious presence, and filled with bright hopes of the better life. My joy was not ecstatic. It was perfectly satisfactory to feel that, "though my heart and flesh fail," God would be "the strength of my heart, and my portion forever." And now, though but partially recovered and still a cripple, with but faint prospect of ever recovering health beyond its present state, I am *calm, peaceful, hopeful,* and, I think, *resigned* to my lot. I greatly marvel that such a poor and unworthy sinner, though saved through infinite grace in Jesus Christ from the guilt of sin by

pardoning mercy, can thus be kept from de-
sponding feelings. I attribute all to the special
care of Him who tenderly puts "underneath
me his everlasting arms" of love and mercy.
In my physical prostration and earthly unfa-
vorable prospects I can truly say,

> "The day glides sweetly o'er my head,
> Made up of innocence and love;
> And soft and silent as the shade
> My nightly minutes gently move.
>
> I often look to the heavenly hills,
> Where groves of living pleasures grow,
> And longing hopes and cheerful smiles
> Sit undisturbed upon my brow."

What a contrast between this and the experience of forty years ago! I was then in perfect
health, of buoyant spirits, full of courage, and
with bright earthly hopes. But I was full, also,
of religious doubts and fears. From a stern
sense of duty I was a preacher of the Gospel,
although the power of that Gospel had, as
yet, not been clearly revealed to my youthful
heart. Now, under these changed and naturally depressing circumstances, I can feel to
"rejoice in the Lord, be patient in tribulation,
and can

> Read my title clear
> To mansions in the skies.'"

Does the reader ask, Through what means and instrumentalities has come about this great change ? I answer, By the grace of God in Christ, through Methodism. I would give due credit to other orthodox Churches for many excellent sentiments and beautiful examples of deep Christian experience and exalted virtues, which have their salutary influence on others, but *I* needed the benefit of the Methodistic doctrines of free grace, of present free and full salvation, a knowledge of present, acceptance with God, and "full assurance of hope" to meet my special necessities. I needed the soul-stirring hymns, the earnest, importunate prayers, the hearty responsive shouts of praise to God, the clear testimonies of love to him, and the wide-awake, free, social means of grace of Methodism to help me into the deeper waters of life than I had heretofore fathomed.

I might have reached this better state of Christian experience elsewhere as well as with the Methodists ; but there would have been more danger of "groping my way" to the better land, only "hoping I had a hope," and feeling the extreme danger of "being deceived," and shuddering at hearing any one say, "I know whom I have believed," than in the good old Bible testimony I have so often heard among

my own people, such as "His Spirit witnesseth
with our spirit that we are the children of God."
"We know we have passed from death unto life,
because we love the brethren." And then those
good old hymns,.such as—

> "My God is reconciled;
> His pard'ning voice I hear:
> He owns *me* for his child;
> *I* can no longer fear:
> With confidence I now draw nigh,
> And Father, Abba, Father, cry."

And this—

> "Exults our rising soul,
> Disburdened of her load,
> And swells, *unutterably full*
> *Of glory* and *of God.*"

Thus have I been led along by the Hand
divine, cheered and confirmed in experience,
comforted and aided by prayers of faith and
deeds of love, in sickness and health, succored
in trials and victorious in conflicts, through the
instrumentalities, associations, and influences
of Methodism, for these forty years past. To
God, in Jesus Christ, and *to him alone*, will·I
ascribe all the praise.

CHAPTER II.

Class-Meetings Forty Years Ago and Now.

———

METHODISM began with class-meetings, and they have proved to be our great nurseries of piety, a leading element of success. Forty years ago, except in more compact places, as in cities and villages, it required great effort to sustain them. As the members were scattered over a region of several miles around, they could not meet without making special effort ; but they enjoyed their meetings all the more for their painstaking.

In many country classes they were obliged to reserve the privileges of class till the days of the pastor's lecture appointments, once in two weeks in those sections of the circuits where most of the members resided, and then meet after the more public services. In other places they met at noon on the Sabbath, or after the afternoon public services closed ; but whenever or wherever class-meetings were held in those days they were, with rare exceptions, seasons of special interest and of much profit to the attendants.

It seems to some of us who used to attend them that the conversational style of conducting them, as then practiced, between leaders and members with reference to personal experience and the practice and growth of Christian virtues, was a very valuable characteristic of class-meetings.

Not unfrequently difficulties between members were settled, unworthy ones excluded from society, probationers received into full member-ship, and as a general rule it was pretty accurately ascertained that our people valued or undervalued class attendance very nearly in proportion to their state of religious interest.

We used to hear objections brought against them by people outside of Methodism. One quality of people, who, if pious at all, possessed it only in a low degree, never saying any thing, or the next thing thereto, on the subject of their own experience or Christian progress, were quite forward in their opposition to them. Their main objection was this : " *Class-meetings are too much like the Romish confessional.* The members are sharply questioned by the leader, to whom they must make confession of their shortcomings and unworthiness, and ask his prayers on their behalf for pardon and salvation." An objection too ridiculous to need refutation.

Another objection came from a very different source, and was of an opposite kind. "*Class-meetings are too exclusive.* People who are not members are prohibited by Discipline from attending more than twice or thrice unless they become members. Now," they used to say, "if these are good meetings, why not open the doors wide enough to admit any who may be disposed to attend them?"

Our answer was: "Class-meetings are for class-members, and the open doors proposed would thwart their design by admitting such as are not in sympathy with us, and perhaps real enemies of the cause of Christ." Other objections were sometimes urged in those days, but they did not militate against the cause to its special detriment.

Many interesting reminiscences might be recorded of class-meetings, especially as connected with our early ministry, from among which we select the following:

In a certain Vermont station, where our young people were gay, social, and joyous, more inclined to sinful amusements than to religion, though constant Church-goers·and Bible-class scholars, we were sometimes annoyed by their thoughtless manners in the Sabbath evening prayer-meetings. At length, by the advice of brethren, the class-meeting was changed to Sabbath evening instead of the prayer-meeting, and the prayer-meeting was appointed for the evening of class-meeting, and in its stead. This was to be only a temporary arrangement, and to be tried as an experiment to break up the annoyances complained of. Our young friends saw the point aimed at, and on the. evening appointed for prayer were out in good numbers. At the Sabbath evening class-meeting some twenty of them were on hand in high glee for a good time. The pastor explained to them the nature and design of class-meetings, and that all present would be expected to kneel in prayer-time, and all would be spoken to separately on the subject of religion, and when addressed each would be expected to rise up and give respectful answers to questions propounded, and speak in appropriate language in regard to their personal interest in matters of religion, and that in no instance had we ever known a gentleman or lady to refuse to comply with such reasonable requests when respectfully presented and understood. How the jolly young company of class-attendants received the instructions we

were somewhat in doubt. It was enough for
me to know they all knelt in prayer-time, and
when spoken to, as others were, each aróse and
gave in respectful language responses to what
was said to them, and received our advice with
apparent seriousness. Some spoke with tremu-
lous voices and tearful eyes ; a few wept, con-
.fessed, asked for the prayers of the class,
sought and found the Saviour, and in due time
joined the Church, which thus assisted them in
· starting in the better way. Their attendance
at that class-meeting, if designed for evil, was
overruled for good.

Of those earlier days in class-meeting experience was reference to a good and faithful
class-leader. On a certain evening, though
usually prompt, he was late to class. He soon
explained to us the cause of his tardiness. He
said, " I had been working in my barn, and was
anxious to close up a certain piece of work before dark ; but along in the afternoon I began
to think that I must give up attending my class
in the evening. I soon met with an accident,
which seemed to say to me, '*Go to class-meeting.*'
But," said he, " ' I *can't* go because I am so hin-
dered.' Awhile after, when hurrying my work

along, my sleigh, which had been carefully placed on a platform over the floor, came down with a crash and was damaged, seeming to say, 'Go to class-meeting, then.' I thought," said he, "it is of no use to try to save time by the neglect of Christian duties, so I left all and hastened to class-meeting."

Experience and observation both are wit-. nesses that his was a wise and safe conclusion, as illustrated in

ANOTHER SINGULAR INCIDENT.

In a certain pastoral charge, when giving out for class-meeting in haying time, I related to the people somewhat of the experience of my good class-leader just referred to, and suggested, if the day should be a good one for haying, some of my brethren might be tempted to stay away, and cautioned them against yielding to the temptation, but to plan their work so as to "go to class-meeting," otherwise something might turn up to hinder them as much as the time it would require to attend it.

My good Brother P. heard the caution with interest, but probably without confidence in my inferences drawn from it. The day came—a bright day for hay-makers. My good Brother P. and hired man were in the field, near the

hour of the appointed meeting, doubtless thinking of class-meeting which they concluded not
to attend, when by a *strange* mishap the usually
good driver drove his team too near a stump
and broke the cart-tongue. My good Brother P.
hearing the noise of breaking exclaimed, "'*Well,
go to class-meeting, then!*' There," said he in
an instant more, "*don't tell Brother Culver of it
for any thing!*" The hired man, also a member of the class, thinking it a little too good to,
keep, took pleasure in telling of it. Now, we
do not say these occurrences came to pass because of the intention to save time by neglect
of duties; but we do believe that, as a rule,
such efforts for the world, to the neglect of plain
and positive religious duties, will bring upon
him who attempts them, in one way or another,
great loss in a worldly sense.

Class-meetings, now in·their one hundred and
sixth year in America and their one hundred and
forty-third in England, may have lost some of
their former valuable characteristics, but they
have outlived all opposition; and, retaining all
the more essential qualities of the early past,
and adding thereto what experience and observation seem to demand by the changed
circumstances of the times, they possess to-day
more than their youthful vigor and success, in

some respects at least. They have better accommodations in class-rooms or other commodious places, and larger attendance. None now molest their devotions. The demand for closed doors, if ever necessary, is now among the things of the past. Class-meetings will continue to be, as they ever have been, among the most efficient means of grace for the building up of believers and the salvation of sinners, through the merits of our Lord Jesus Christ, to whom be the glory now and forever.

Some other denominations of evangelical Christians, seeing their value, not only cease their opposition, but, so far as their ecclesiastical organisms will allow, have adopted them in *name,** or, under *another name*, have adopted their main characteristics.

May class-meetings, by whatsoever name they may be called, and by whomsoever held, become more and more the means of saving souls, and God be glorified!

* Class-meetings are known to be held in some of our Freewill Baptist Churches.

CHAPTER III.

Circuits, Stations, and Salaries Then and Now.

CIRCUITS THEN AND STATIONS NOW.

THE circuit system was a favorite one with Methodism from its origin. For many years these circuits were very large, extending over many towns, and sometimes as large as a modern presiding elder's district. Forty years ago they were much reduced in size, especially in New England, embracing only some three or four towns, with only some four, five, or six Sabbath preaching-places, as convenience or necessity required. To each of these fields of labor there were usually appointed a preacher in charge and one or two colleagues, who were generally juniors in years and in experience, all of whom usually went with cheerfulness to their work, under the care and guidance of Christ, "the Chief Shepherd," to look after the flock, which was scattered along the valleys and among the mountains of their widely-extended circuits.

The amount of labor required was, of course, very great. No less than two hundred sermons must be preached during the year, nor less than this number of class and prayer-meetings attended during the time ; and no less than a thousand family visits made, requiring as many as two thousand miles' travel in a year. These reminiscences of forty years ago I take from recorded facts, kept by myself, of my own labors in those early times.

The mode of traveling, especially by the junior preachers, was on horseback, with *saddle-bags* for carrying our reading-books and needed change of apparel, and on our longer routes, frequently with our *umbrellas* and *rolled-up overcoats* strapped to our saddles.

Some of us were often taken, when among strangers, to be *doctors*, (not *D. D.'s* but *M. D.'s* —doctors of divinity were scarce in those days,) as our mode of conveyance and saddle-bags were, in outside appearance, not dissimilar to theirs. Such mistakes, though innocently made and generally harmless, were nevertheless occasionally quite troublesome. The trouble of being hailed as *doctors*, to inquire after sick folks, was small compared with some others. I will illustrate my meaning by relating an incident in my own early history in the ministry.

On a certain circuit, not many miles from old "Dartmouth Medical College," I chanced to put up for the night at the house of one of my parishioners, where, being a new-comer on the circuit, I was mostly a stranger in his neighborhood. Learning that there was to be a funeral of a young lady that forenoon, and as I was to pass along that way, I concluded to loiter a little in order to attend it. On arriving at the house where death had entered I learned that I was too early for the funeral, so I passed on to another part of my circuit, not supposing I had done any harm.

A few days after I was surprised to learn that they had taken me to be a young doctor, or a "Hanoverian Medic," out on an excursion for *robbing grave-yards of their sacred dead* to take to their *dissecting-rooms;* and lest that new grave should be disturbed, it had been vigilantly watched by the troubled neighbors for several nights in succession after the burial, who, doubtless, pronounced their *solemn anathemas* against any young *doctor* or despicable Hanover "Medic" who should be mean enough to want to *rob a grave-yard* of its sacred dead !

How they felt when they learned the facts I cannot *state*, but the reader can *guess*.

This horseback mode of travel, nevertheless, was the best adapted to all the "highways" and "byways" which led to the homes of our people who lived in the back towns and rural districts of our circuits. The married preachers, as now, lived in parsonages, or more generally, like Paul, in "their own *hired* houses," but were necessarily absent on their large circuits most of their time. A single man in those days, with rare exceptions, had "no certain abiding-place;" a regular boarding-place for him was out of the question. He went "from house to house," in the different parts of his work, seldom staying two nights in succession in the same house.

This was my experience for nearly the first four years of my ministry. My temporary stopping-places, not to say homes, were so arranged in the different parts of my circuit as to bring me on Saturday night into the immediate region of my Sabbath meeting, where I kept my needed change of raiment for the Sabbath. These places of entertainment were freely opened to me, where I spent many happy hours.

Should the following reminiscences prove distasteful to the reader, I hope he will pardon me for their introduction here. They give some of the *unpleasant* phases of itinerant life forty years ago.

FREE ENTERTAINMENT, BUT DISAGREEABLE FARE.

Having a lecture appointment among entire strangers some fifteen miles away, in an obscure town among the mountains, I went and preached. When the meeting was through, a man some fifty years old, I should judge, came to me and kindly invited me to his house for entertainment for the night. I gladly accepted the invitation, and went in company with him to his home. On the way he pointed out to me various objects of interest to himself, mostly such as pertained to his own property, saying, " *This* is *my* sawmill;" " *This* is *my* farm ;" and at length, " *This* is my house," intending, as I thought, to impress me favorably with reference to his financial circumstances.

The house was a little old log hut, near which were one or two large barns, and all the way between the buildings was the barn-yard, and a large stock of cattle, equally in the door-yard as in the barn-yard, and a running brook passing through, *equally* accommodating the occupants of the house and barn with its richly-colored waters.

It being in the month of April, "the sight of my eyes had an effect on my heart" not very cheering. "Here," said the good man of the house, "this is where I live; walk in, and we will take care of your horse." While yet in the yard I saw a tall, awkward, and foolish-appearing youth come out of the house with a pail in his hand, (*it looked like a slop-pail,*) who rushed to the brook and dipped up a pailful of the polluted water. I entered the house, and soon saw the tea-kettle *filled with it* for tea, and put over the fire in the open fire-place to heat. Not being anxious for *tea* just then, I excused myself as best I could, and asked for *bread and milk.* The request was reluctantly granted.

In due time there was brought to my lap an old three-pint tin dish, which contained a rusty iron spoon and a full supply of clammy brown bread and milk, which milk was fresh from the *untidy milk pail.* Attempting to eat, my appetite utterly failed me. I *just then* did not feel to relish bread and milk. I again excused myself from eating in the best way I knew how, and set up the dish. At length bedtime came. I was assigned to the bed in the only room down stairs, that same old kitchen. The family —not a small one—retired somewhere, to the chamber or barn, or somewhere else; at any rate all disappeared for the night except one son, who was to be my bed-fellow. The bed clothing was uncleanly, ragged, and of unpleasant flavor. I sighed, prayed, dozed, and longed for day-dawn. Morning came. I was an early riser for once, at least. The family appearing again, the breakfast was fast being prepared, when I noticed the tea-kettle was filled with water from the same pail as the night before, and the potatoes put over the fire to boil with water from the same source. Two johnny-cakes on wooden plates were baking before the fire. Thus progressing was the breakfast when the foolish son, returning from the aforesaid yard, having stepped where he ought not, sat down on the hearthstone a little too near the baking johnny-cakes.

At the breakfast-table my usually good appetite somehow failed me. The tea I could not drink, the potatoes I could not eat, the johnny-cakes I could not touch. I excused myself from eating again as best I could. After prayers I bade them good-bye, and after riding some ten miles I called at a good farm-house, where resided one of our best Methodist families. On reporting where I was from, and where I stayed the night before, the good woman, knowing the family, immediately said, " I think then by this time that you are hungry," and without further ceremony provided me with food, which I thankfully received and was satisfied.

The next year I chanced to relate my adventure to my senior preacher, and he followed it with this story of his own experience : "A few years ago," said he, "I stayed in that same house, slept in that same room, and, I presume, in that same bed. Before retiring that same man said to me, ' We have *fleas* here. I do not know as you are acquainted with such annoyances. They *may* trouble you. They used to trouble me once, but I have got used to them, and learned how to get along with them better than I once did. I think of Daniel in the *lions' den*, and pray to the God of Daniel to give me grace to endure their *bite*, and now get along quite comfortably with them.' "

My good itinerant brother continued his story by saying, " I soon had occasion to think of ' the God of Daniel,' but endured the night as best I could. I arose in the morning at day-dawn, shook the fleas from my clothes as well as I could in the open air, caught my horse, and took my departure probably long before the family were up, glad to get off with so near a whole skin as I did, and left them to wonder what had become of me."

Such were some of the annoyances of some
of our stopping-places under the old circuit system ; but we had far more agreeables to praise
God for than disagreeables to sigh over, and
even these were often turned to a good account,
for we were the more thankful for the good enjoyed, and sought for more grace to endure the
occasional unpleasant circumstances we en-
countered.

The old circuit system has gradually passed
away, having yielded to the modern demand for
stations. Methodism has left the backgrounds
to a great extent and moved into the centers of
population and influence. The pastoral charges,
even their outer limits, are now within a few
miles, as a general thing, of the pastor's home,
saving him the trouble and expense of keeping
a horse and carriage to reach the farthest members of his congregations. He can, with better
economy, hire, as occasion may require, or walk
to the homes of most of his parishioners.

Thus the pleasant parsonage and happy home
of the preacher can be more constantly enjoyed.
The time and chances for pulpit preparation are
hereby greatly enhanced, and not .more than
half as many sermons have to be preached as
on the old circuit plan ; but, notwithstanding
this, pastoral labors, social meetings, and many

Church benevolent enterprises, and the thousand and one various stirring events of the day, in which he ought and *must* take part, will keep his utmost powers upon their full stretch, increasing the anxieties, cares, and labors of the preacher of to-day even above those of forty years ago.

There are some things in the change from the old circuit plan and the adoption of the modern stationing system which are to be deplored. One thing in particular deserves specially to be named. The feeble societies of the more rural towns, for want of proper pastoral care, are constantly growing weaker, and how to provide for them is now an important practical question.

The friends of the cause in those places are not able to support constant preaching. The Missionary Society has not the funds to spare for all such calls, and yet the people of these places need the means of grace.

The question still presses itself upon thoughtful minds, What shall be done for them? Some of our wisest and most practical men are of the opinion that the only remedy for these weak portions of our Zion is the re-adoption of the old circuit plan for *them*, while we retain for *most* of our work the *present stationing system.*

"Wisdom is profitable to direct." May God give the needed wisdom to his Church, that she may devise the plan and execute the work which will produce the greatest good to the greatest number !

We will next compare our preachers'

SALARIES THEN AND NOW.

The disciplinary claim for a single man forty years ago was $100 and his traveling expenses. For a married man, for self and wife, $200 and traveling expenses, then understood to mean for moving bills and horse-shoeing. For children under fourteen years of age it was $16 each, and for minors over fourteen years, $24. Seldom was this small claim received.

It is presumed that in New England not more than one half of this amount on an average was paid them.

My first appointment was under the presiding elder for three months, to fill out the conference year, where the junior preacher's health had failed. The preacher in charge was one of the most popular preachers in the conference, and the circuit a full average one for support.

The time of service, the last quarter in the year, being ended, a disciplinary division of receipts gave me the sum of $13, which I most

4

gladly accepted, it being the first money I ever received for preaching.

In 1833, the next year, I joined the New Hampshire Conference, and was appointed to the circuit in the bounds of which I had spent all my early days. This was regarded as an average one for support. In this I received my disciplinary proportion paid in, and it amounted to $53 for one year's service.

The next year, on a laborious circuit, with a sickly preacher in charge, which added much to my labors, I also shared my proportion with him, which amounted, all told, to $47.

I am confident that these receipts are equal, with rare exceptions, to the average amounts of other preachers, who were similarly stationed in those days. A small support, it is true, not adequate to meet our real needs ; but we had souls for our hire, and, thus encouraged, were content to wait for better days. We seldom heard the subject of small salaries alluded to by the preachers, or any complaint of hard fare.

Now, after forty years, the Church, having greatly increased in numbers and wealth, and having been better instructed in the duty of supporting the Gospel ministry, has a better record.

The old disciplinary allowance of salaries, which long since became obsolete, is expunged from the Discipline. That station is now considered very poor or exceedingly penurious which asks for and receives a preacher without paying him a fair salary.

Take, as an illustration, the receipts of salaries for 1872 in the New Hampshire Conference, scarce an average conference for supporting their pastors. The whole number of effective ministers was ninety-one. Of these twenty-seven received salaries ranging from $1,000 to $2,000, and twenty-one salaries' ranging from $700 to $1,000 ; while thirty-two acknowledged receipts ranging from $500 to $700, leaving only eight who received from $400 to $500, and only one less than $400. Some of the last-named sums were paid for only partial pastoral services to feeble men, or those living out of the bounds of their charges, who in part depended on other means of support.

These figures may appear very small in the estimation of some, but are a great advance on receipts of earlier days. That preacher must be a poor economist who cannot live, extraordinaries excepted, on salaries now generally received. If he needs better pay he should make his wants known, and show by faithful labors that he deserves it, and doubtless it will be forthcoming.

It may appear surprising to some of our youthful readers that preachers were not better supported in those earlier days ; but those who are familiar with the financial circumstances of our people in those times, and their denominational and social surroundings, can see quite clearly the cause.

While some of our members and supporters were possessed of moderate wealth, and paid liberally toward supporting the Gospel, there were others who had never been properly educated to do for this cause "as God had prospered them."

But most of our people were poor, and those who contributed liberally according to their means could do but little ; nevertheless it must be confessed that there were some men of property then, as now, who were so penurious that they did little or nothing financially to aid the cause of God.

The following will illustrate the liberal ideas and generous impulses of *some* men who lived *then* and a few *others* who live *now*.

Having nearly completed my term of service on a certain station near forty years ago, I made my final call, as pastor, on a family not mem-

bers of my Church, but of my congregation.
They were comparatively wealthy. I had passed
some rods from the house when the owner and
occupant of the premises, who was at work by
the roadside, called to me to know how I was
coming out on support, and said as he had paid
nothing he wanted to do something, and as he
must hasten his work along, asked me to go
back to tell his wife to hand me a *ninepence* toward my salary. Not feeling like returning for
that purpose, I went on my way thinking, "What
ninepenny men some mortals are!"

A GOOD PRACTICAL LESSON FROM DEAR-BOUGHT EXPERIENCE.

I will give an early incident of being on a
journey minus money in my purse, a thing to
which I was sometimes subjected, with the
alternative of staying at home.

I had occasion to travel some thirty miles
away, and before returning had been obliged to
empty my pockets of money for the purchase
of some needed books. On my way back I
planned to stop over night, some fifteen or
twenty miles from my parish, with a Methodist
preacher, (all our preachers kept open doors for
each other in those days,) where I anticipated a
hearty welcome and a good visit. I reached

the place about dark, tired and hungry ; but, to my great discomfiture, the doors were closed and the family away.   The evenings were short, and I, among strangers, without supper, money, or lodgings, must do quickly *something* with myself for the night.   What that *something* should be I at first could not tell ; but I soon thought of a well-to-do, influential class-leader, whom I had a few times met, and who was well spoken of by those who knew him.   I went to his door and rang the bell, when the following conversation occurred while I was *outside* and he still *in bed:*

"Who is there ?"

I gave my name.

"What do you want ?"

"I want to put up with you for the night."

"Haven't got any horse-keeping."

"I can go to the stable with my *horse* if you can keep *me.*"

To this he reluctantly consented.

I went to the stable with my horse, returned and rang the bell again.   "Mine host" responded to the call by rising from bed and lighting a lamp.   He came to the door without *dressing* himself, and escorted me quite unceremoniously to my lodging-room, asking me no questions about health or supper or any thing else.

Every circumstance combined to make me wakeful, thoughtful, and uneasy; among these were *no welcome, no supper,* (a small item in the programme,) *no money,* and, withal, no sleep. How shall I pay my horse-keeping bill? was the plague of my thoughts. Morning coming, I in due time presented my jaded self to the family.

The good class-leader had by this time come to himself enough to offer as good an apology as he could for his treatment of the previous evening, namely, " He had gone to *bed,* and was *tired* and *sleepy.*" I accepted his apology very cheerfully, and was kindly treated.

It was rather a strait place for me to tell him I was *out of money,* and should be obliged to ask him to *lend* me some to pay for *horse-keeping.* But I did it, and he readily complied.

I thanked them for their hospitality, bade them good-bye, paid ·my bill at the stable, and went on my way rejoicing that I fared so much · better than my Master, "who had not where to lay his head."

In a few weeks I saw "mine host" again, and offered him the amount I borrowed, but he decidedly declined it. I learned a good practical lesson from this somewhat "dear-bought" experience, namely, *Either to stay at home, or never to start on another journey without money enough in my pocket to pay for "supper" and "horse-keeping."*

CHAPTER IV.

Quarterly Meetings Then and Now.

A S our circuits in those days embraced several towns, and had the services of two or more preachers, our presiding elders' districts, though large in territory, included within their bounds only about one quarterly meeting for each Sabbath of the quarter. Extraordinaries excepted, the presiding elder therefore attended four quarterly meetings for each pastoral charge during the conference year. These meetings were generally seasons of special interest. The brethren and sisters of the Church came in from different parts of the circuit on Saturday P.M., the distant ones to tarry through the meeting. After the presiding elder had preached a good practical sermon the preacher in charge proceeded to invite those desiring entertainment, and those who would open their doors to entertain, to tarry to make the necessary distribution. Usually a goodly number of both kinds readily reported themselves.

This service ended, then came the quarterly conference, with all its important business matters, to take the time and attention of the official members for some time longer, the records of which were then, as now, taken down by a secretary appointed at the time for the purpose, who afterward delivered them over to the recording stewards for record ; but their books, in too many instances, give but a poor showing of the doings of said conferences, a failure greatly to be regretted by all interested in the important Methodistic history of those earlier times.

The Saturday evening prayer-meetings were usually held in different neighborhoods, and, with the additional help from abroad, were seasons of great interest. The Sabbath morning love-feast, especially, was a time of great " refreshing from the presence of the Lord."

Special attention was paid to the time of opening and closing the doors according to previous notice, and a preacher during the time was stationed at the door to guard it from intruders. " Strangers," that is, those not members, were not permitted to attend more than "twice or thrice, unless they became members." Also, those who adorned their person with gold or other gay ornaments were prohibited, by the rules of the Church, from entering.

Love-feast ending, one of the circuit-preach-
ers conducted the public exercises and preached
the morning sermon. The afternoon sermon,
extraordinaries excepted, was preached by the
presiding elder. Then followed the sacrament
of the Lord's Supper, a season of special profit,
as the members from different parts of the
charge once more communed together at the
table of their common Lord and Master. This
was followed by an appropriate exhortation to
faithfulness by the presiding elder, and sometimes by a season of prayer for souls seeking
salvation, who had come by invitation to the
altar, and not unfrequently by the testimonies
of *victory* in the name of the Lord from those
who thus came. Such was an "old-fashioned
quarterly meeting" of forty or more years ago.

Reference has been made to the custom of
guarding the love-feast door. This old disciplinary rule, in some places, had then lost
some of its practical significance, but was not
wholly obsolete in many other parts of our
Church.

To that *very important post* of ministerial
duty I was sometimes put in trust. On one
occasion, I particularly remember, I criticised
sharply a stranger several years my senior who
had presented himself for admission, whom I at

length found to be a Methodist preacher. His
apology for so long keeping dark, he said, "was
to test the fidelity of the young preacher in
charge of the door." In pleasant terms he has
often since referred me to this our first interview.

What changes in regard to these meetings in
the space of the past forty years! Our work
now being cut up into stations, and our New
England districts embracing three or four times
the number of the Sabbaths in a quarter, our
presiding elders are obliged to divide the work
of their Sabbaths between two or more accessible appointments, and at this rapid rate be
present on the Sabbath only some twice in the
year. The Saturday afternoon sermon is now
seldom preached. The Saturday evening
prayer-meeting is only the usual one. The
"love-feast," if held at all, is not enlivened by
testimonies or persons from abroad, though
often a season of good religious interest, but
far from the " old-style " in its testimony and
power.

For these changes, as our work is now arranged into stations and districts, there is no
apparent remedy. We must take matters as
they are, and as present circumstances seem to
necessitate.

We are not sure but these changes from "old-fashioned quarterly meetings," in which we reluctantly lose some valuable usages, are more than compensated by the gain we make in more constant means of grace, more constant watch-care of pastors, and by the average value of our more efficient and frequent social meetings.

The custom of guarding the love-feast door, if ever a necessity, is now among the things the need of which has passed away.

We are seldom now imposed upon by ill-disposed persons in attendance. Few except our own people now attend our "love-feasts," and when they do it is with good intent. These meetings, with less guarded doors and less attendance from abroad, continue to be rich "feasts of love" to all such as truly "hunger and thirst after righteousness."

Though customs change in respect to our quarterly meetings and "love-feasts," may all the real essentials of our Church customs and power never become obsolete or lose their powerful charms!

CHAPTER V.

Methodistic Customs and Characteristics.

STYLE OF DRESS THEN AND NOW.

THE style of dress with the male lay-membership of our Church was not essentially different from that of other men similarly situated in social life. But there was a marked difference in the style of our ministers' apparel. With rare exceptions, they dressed their necks with the white handkerchief, minus the collar, then the only and almost sure badge of a Methodist minister. The custom went so far that when a young man obtained license to exhort, the next thing expected was to see him in this style of neck-dress.

The departure from this old custom by any of our preachers, old or young, was regarded as an unfortunate departure from the "ancient landmarks." Even a young minister would feel not a little afflicted to learn that any brother minister had exchanged this peculiar badge for the more common style of neck-dress. But innovations on old customs, when once commenced, often have a wide and rapid spread. It was so with this.

I have now in my mind the expressions of sadness uttered to me some thirty-five years ago, when I first made this change. A preacher of my age seriously lectured me for my worldly conformity and departure from old Methodistic usage. But the grief of my good brother was soon assuaged. In less than twelve months he followed what he so recently had so seriously felt to be a bad example. Thus one after another departed from this old custom, until there can now scarcely be one found, from senior bishop to exhorter, in all our borders, who clings to this once popular usage, and the change does not seem to produce any disastrous results.

There were once other characteristics in the dress of our ministers, such as the wide-brimmed hat and round-breasted coat and vest, but they were gradually going out of use forty years ago. Though worn by some, they were not strenuously insisted upon as a rule for others. Now they are seldom worn— never by any except a few aged ministers who still linger among us as reporters of the long gone-by.

The sisters of the Church gave good heed

to our old Methodistic rules on dress. Setting
out in the divine life as Bible Christians, they
could not overlook the divine prohibition of all
gaudiness and extravagance, and adopted a
plain, economical habit, traces of which are still
seen in our ranks. They gave good heed to the
apostolic rule, " Whose adorning let it not be
that outward adorning of *plaiting the hair*, and
of *wearing of gold*, or of putting on of [super-
fluous] apparel ; but the hidden man of the
heart, even the ornament of a meek and quiet
spirit, which is in the sight of God of great
price."

There has since come a change. The plain,
old-fashioned Methodistic bonnet has seldom
been seen for years. The modest style of their
other apparel has been exchanged for the more
common fashions of the world, or, perhaps more
properly, like other Christian women of the
present day. This change may be, perhaps,
accounted for as follows. Some years since
plainness in female attire became the prevailing fashion of all the ladies of the country.
Plain Methodistic bonnets and dresses were
then in the height of fashion, and continued so
for some time. The female members of our
Church were then, in their style of dress, like
the world without conforming to it ; the world

conformed to them. At length, when the fashion changed again from plain to more ornamental, our sisters very naturally, but almost unconsciously, changed with it. Though less Methodistic according to old ideas, yet we trust there are some still among us who deplore the prevailing extravagant fashions of our times, and intend to conform to apostolic and Methodistic rules "in modest apparel."

Our members, male and female, should be plain and modest in their apparel, in defiance against the world, and as examples worthy of imitation—not odd enough to attract particular attention, or so coarse or untasteful as to merit disgust. "Cleanliness, simplicity, economy, and modesty," says a certain writer, "are Christian virtues, without which our piety will appear deformed, and lose much of its influence both on ourselves and others."

PUBLIC LAY TESTIMONY FOR CHRIST

Was a custom commonly practiced by our brethren and sisters in public on the Sabbath and other occasions in those early days. One or more—frequently several—would arise in their places and testify to the truth just preached, relate experience, or engage in earnest exhortation, often to the edification of the Church and profit of others.   But, unfortunately, some instances would occur when the style and spirit of their testimony would prove worse than a failure in their influence on the hearers.   It diverted attention from the word preached by wearisome length or indiscreet utterances.

In my early ministry I was invariably in the habit of giving "liberty" for brethren and sisters to speak after sermon, and often heard *powerful* testimonies for Christ in our Sabbath assemblies.   I *sometimes* heard testimonies which were apparently *worse* than profitless. Such testimonies were the exceptions, not the more common ones.   We praise the great Head of the Church for the good resulting from this old custom in many instances.

This practice has now become obsolete.   If ever there was a demand for it, that demand has passed away.   Our stated Sabbath evening prayer-meetings are within the reach of nearly all who attend worship during the day, where their testimony for Christ is urged and expected, and can be generally given without interrupting or delaying the appropriate services. We, who have been familiar with this old custom of earlier times, part with it without remorse of conscience or tears of sorrow for its termination, praying that the genuine "old-fashioned" testimony for Christ, in the *social* worship of God, may become more and more the custom of all Methodists, as well as of all of every name, till the coming of the Lord to gather his people home.

Another custom of forty years ago was that of

KNEELING IN TIME OF PUBLIC AND SOCIAL PRAYER.

This custom has high authority, derived from the precepts and examples of the word of God. It received the hearty sanction of the Church of England, and of the early Methodist fathers. They heeded the injunction of Holy Writ, "Come, let us bow down and worship, let us *kneel* before the Lord our Maker." For "at the name of Jesus every *knee* should bow, and every tongue confess."

The Methodists forty years ago kept up this practice, and continued it till some years later in New England. And we are happy to add, we have seen it practiced, in recent years, in the South and West, and even in the western part of New England. But we are sorry to record the fact, that in very many places the practice has been of late abandoned in public worship except by the minister, and is too little heeded except by a few in social worship. We should love the "old landmarks which the fathers have set," especially when they have been set with unerring accuracy by the hand of Divine Wisdom.

AUDIBLE RESPONSES THEN AND NOW.

Appropriate responses in public prayer, and other religious exercises, have been common in all ages, both among Jews and Christians. The Church of England, and the Protestant Episcopal Church in America, in their prayer-books and by example, give the practice their emphatic approval. Our Methodistic fathers were, therefore, by inheritance, entitled to the custom, and faithfully continued to give their audible responses.

Forty years ago such utterances as "Amen," "Glory to God," "Halleluia," were not unfrequent in our social and public worship. There were then, as now, different temperaments and tastes. Some from full hearts "shouted aloud the praises of the Lord," and felt the better for the privilege enjoyed; while others, of cooler temperament, chose only to employ their hearty "Amens" in approval of the truths which were being uttered. Still others, though not shouters themselves, were never annoyed at hearing good Christian people " shout aloud the praises of the Lord." A fourth class, of very sensitive nerves and delicate ears, were unedified, and apparently unprofited, hearers of such responses, but generally, for the sake of the cause they loved, were not " troublers of our Israel " on this account.

The appellation of " noisy, shouting Methodist." was then not an uncommon one. Our young people now are less accustomed to shouting themselves, or of hearing it from others ; and our older members, once so accustomed to it, now, for the sake of others, restrain their emotions. Nevertheless, even now are often heard these old-fashioned responses in social and public worship in some parts of our Zion.

The authority for such responsive utterances is from the highest source. When David closed his psalm at the removal of the ark, " All the people said *Amen*, and praised the Lord." St. Paul, in urging the importance of speaking understandingly in public, inquires, " How shall he that occupieth the room of the unlearned say *Amen* at thy giving of thanks ? seeing he understandeth not what thou sayest."

At the dedication of the Temple, when God appeared in his cloud of glory, the people " bowed themselves to the ground, and praised

the Lord, saying, For he is good ; for his mercy
endureth forever." When Jesus rode in tri-
umph into Jerusalem. his disciples, unrebuked,
shouted " *Hosanna:* blessed is he that cometh
in the name of the Lord. *Hosanna in the
highest !* " At the laying of the foundation of
the Temple " the people shouted with a great
shout, and praised the Lórd."

A practice of such high authority our people
should not then be either ashamed nor afraid
to indorse practically.

May all the essentials of worshiping " God in
spirit and in truth " never cease among us, but
increase more and more till that glorious day
when the " great multitude, which no man can
number," shall be gathered " from the east and
the west, from the north and the south, and
shall sit down with Abraham, Isaac, and Jacob
in the kingdom of heaven," and all in blessed
harmony shout aloud their praises to God and
the " Lamb, who has redeemed them and washed
them in his own blood ! "

LOSING STRENGTH ; OR, THE FALLING UNDER
THE POWER OF GOD, SO-CALLED, THEN AND
NOW.

The manifestation bearing this appellation
was not uncommon forty years ago. Often have

I seen persons under a high state of religious emotion fall powerless, physically, and remain so sometimes for hours, with countenances radiant with delight, and their spirits in apparent communion with heaven. When gradually regaining strength they would first, with low and soft voice, and then, as strength increased, utter forth louder praises to God and the Lamb who had given them the victory. These manifestations were occasionally witnessed in class and prayer meetings, and in time of public worship. They were always expected at our campmeetings. I have witnessed them, within forty years, at the family altar of my members, in the house of God on the Sabbath, as well as in the tented grove. I have seen the skeptic look upon the scene in utter amazement, and heard him ask, " What does this all mean ? " Sometimes I have known experiments tried to test whether they were a reality or a pretense ; and many have been constrained to say, " This is the Lord's doings, and it is marvelous in our eyes."

Such manifestations were very common in the days of Wesley and Edwards, as also were other peculiar physical exercises. They were not confined to any denomination, but were doubtless more frequent among the early Methodists.

These manifestations, as years passed on, became less frequent, and have gradually diminished, until now they seldom occur. Were these peculiar manifestations really from God or not? We do not well to doubt their origin. They usually came upon the persons when their minds were drawn toward the divine Spirit with undivided attention, and on their utmost stretch for heavenly things.

Similar instances are recorded in the Word of Life. Such, I judge, was the physical and spiritual condition of Peter, James, and John on the Mount of Transfiguration; of Paul when "caught up to the third heavens, and heard things unlawful for man to utter," but "whether in the body or out of the body he could not tell;" and of the Revelator, John, when on the Isle of Patmos he "fell as a dead man at the feet" of the glorious manifestation of Him "who was the brightness of the Father's glory."

But why are these physical manifestations so seldom now, when once so frequent? The answer to this question, in the opinion of candid minds, is not very easily given. Will it do to say that the faith and piety of the Church have so far abated that God has withdrawn his special presence and favor to the extent that he will not equally commune with us now as then?

This we shall be slow to believe. Unless we grossly misjudge, there is as much consistent, fervent piety in the Methodist Church to-day as there was forty years ago. More than this, the manifestations to which we refer were not wholly confined to the highest type of piety. Many became thus prostrated in strength whose steadfast devotion to the cause of God was not remarkable.

Will it do to regard all these manifestations as the result of nervous excitement or physical ailments? Certainly not. Not only have physically infirm and nervous persons been thus overcome, but men of great physical endurance, and evenly balanced in body and mind, have been under this power. Why, then, have these manifestations so far passed away? Has God changed in his mode of manifestations to us? or have we learned, whether right or wrong, to resist these influences?

Of one thing we are sure. In those early days of precious revivals *worship* was far more *exciting,* affecting the nervous system more than the same degree of piety now under *calmer* and more *enlightened* worship. Whether this is the *real* cause the reader must judge for himself. We know that God *can* and *does* commune with his people, and gloriously carry on his work without these peculiar manifestations; and if he shall continue to withhold them, or again bring them to pass, we will cheerfully say, " He doeth all things well." All glory to his holy name! May the *real strength* of his Church increase more and more until the divine glory shall fill the earth !

CHAPTER VI.

Ministerial "Visiting from House to House"

——•——

THIS duty is most distinctly required of our ministers in the word of God, and by the Discipline of our Church. From the introduction of Methodism it has ever been insisted upon, and to a great extent practiced by her ministry. This was a prominent feature in the practical workings of our Church forty years ago. It has been elsewhere said that ordinarily our ministers made at least one thousand family visits during each conference year. To accomplish this even the preacher needed to average some thirty per week, and more generally perform them in the P.M., omitting, as a rule, the holy Sabbaths and Mondays, not generally appropriate days for ministers or the families of parishioners for such visits. The programme marked out and generally approved for these visits was religious conversation and prayer with the families, varied according to their spiritual condition.

Some made it a rule to talk with each one accessible separately and faithfully, and warn, invite, reprove, encourage, or comfort, as he thought the occasion required, and then pray for them, whether invited or not, if allowed to do so.

Our *wise* and *much* esteemed presiding elder of early times, Rev. J. G. Dow, took occasion at one of our "ministerial associations" to give us young ministers a good talk on the mode of pastoral visiting most proper to be pursued. While he urged faithfulness in the duty, he would have us carefully consider whether the families visited were in proper condition to turn aside from the routine of daily labors and have prayers. He said that "there might be circumstances when it would be exceedingly inappropriate even to *suggest* it, as a family would feel very backward to refuse, and really be harmed to allow it." He gave the following illustration: "A certain Methodist pastor called at the house of one of his parishioners, where the woman was a member of the Church, but her husband not inclined to religion. The good woman was preparing the oven to bake for dinner ; the man of the house was out in the field with hired help, expecting to return for dinner at the appointed hour. Just as the oven was ready for use the good but unobserving minister proposed prayer. The good woman was too *modest* or too *bashful* to decline it. When through, the oven was too cool for baking the needed dinner. When the hungry men came from the field they found a deeply mortified and tortured woman and a raw dinner. The husband was very angry, and the others not very agreeable. That minister might with much propriety have omitted prayer that time, and he should have known it."

Others were more observing, and sought to adapt their visits more to the circumstances of the families they visited ; while still others, as now, doubtless there were who were too willing to find some excuse for their neglect, and either did not visit many of their parishioners at all, or failed to make them appropriately religious.

Some of our pastors, then as now, were careful to visit the people of their own Church and congregation once per quarter, and, extraordinaries excepted, those *only;* while other Methodist pastors, especially where there were not other pastors, felt it to be their duty to visit "from house to house" the *good, bad,* and *indifferent,* passing by none as far as they went.

I confess myself to have been early impressed with this idea by the example of those I had early known, and from my own convictions of duty for the well-being of precious souls who could not be reached so well in any other way. I began my ministry with this view of it. I often in my visits found those who were suffering by bereavements or other domestic afflictions, and needed to be comforted ; those in doubts and fears, who needed encouragement ; those who were cold in religion, and needed reviving ; those awakened, who needed to be led to Christ for salvation ; and the wayward ones, who needed to be reproved and led in the right way. In most such families these calls were duly appreciated, and I trust somewhat profitable ; and when there was no special embarrassment by any peculiar circumstances as above named, our good people, generally with open doors and open arms, received us into their houses, where we were cheerfully entertained and refreshed.

These cheering facts prepare me, and I trust the reader also, for some records of a very opposite character—treatment far more easy to forgive than to forget. I hope the young pastor will be spared the embarrassments of meeting similar receptions, though grace is free and equal to any emergency, and the promise of the Master is, " Lo, I am with you alway."

My first rebuff in the line of visiting as a

minister was in my native town, not many miles from my early home, where I had two winters before taught the district school, and a part of the winter boarded in a family of high respectability, though the husband and father, a rigid Calvinist, was not always amiable, for reasons easily explained by his family, but still a professor of religion. All its members had till a year or two before been members of a Church of the Calvinistic faith. Two maiden daughters, perhaps between thirty and forty years old, of uncommon intelligence, culture, and Christian character, had seen proper to connect themselves with the Methodists, no doubt to the great grief of their bigoted father.

In my early ministry I called again as an acquaintance and friend, and by invitation stopped to dinner. My horse was put into the stable, and I made my visit with the family. After dinner I walked out into the front yard, followed by the old man of the house, who began to question me about my preaching. "You have begun to preach, then, have you?" said he, to which I gave a suitable reply. He immediately added, "If you will preach such doctrine as John Calvin did I shall approve of your course!" I replied, "Shall you not if I preach such doctrine as John Wesley did?"

He quickly responded, with great warmth and strong emphasis, " No ! He was a heretic, and so are all his followers ! " and added, " They will come where they are not *wanted;* they will put their horses in the *barn,* to eat up the hay that don't belong to them ; they will come into people's houses and ' lead away silly women,' and come and *sit* at their tables, and *eat up* their victuals." To all of which I quickly replied, " Mr. C——, if I am an intruder upon your rights I will leave you ! " He then answered, " I respect you as a *young man ;* I value you as our former *school-teacher;* I know and *respect* your father ; but as a *Methodist preacher* I cannot approve of you. You will find the true doctrine to preach in the ninth chapter of Romans ! " It is needless for me to add that the old man and his young intruder were soon at a respectful distance from each other, and that the like intrusion has never been repeated.

Another embarrassing spot I found myself in a few months later was on my first circuit, when I called at the residence of a Universalist family where I sought to be faithful in my visit, as I then (an inexperienced youth in these matters) un—— od duty. I found the woman, who was so—— ixty years old, in her kitchen shelling peas for dinner. I, as easily as I knew how, asked her whether she enjoyed religion. She answered me snappishly, " Yes, I *do!* But I didn't .*go to ministers* for it, either !" and instantly left me alone in the room. But immediately the man of the house came in, and, in a more talkative mood, began conversation, to the great annoyance of his disturbed wife and a proud-spirited son, as evidenced by his coming to the door again and again, saying, " Come, father, didn't you know you ought to be going ?" (it appeared that his horse was at the door for him to ride away somewhere,) and father would answer, " Well, well, son, I will be in time." Again the door would open, and I would hear in *harsh* tones the son's voice, " Come, father, *why don't you start?*" and again the good-natured father would put him off. But the troublesome young Methodist preacher soon relieved the old lady, who had " got her religion without going to ministers after it," and the rest of the equally *pious* family, by taking his departure, which, doubtless, should have been done by him sooner than it was.

In another place I had the whole section within a few miles of the church for m█████sh, where, at that time, there was no othe█████or, and I resolved ónvisiting every family within its limits.

There was one particular family whose immoral qualities were such as to give me and my people no little solicitude regarding the treatment I should receive, as no preacher had ever called there. The whole family were perfectly skeptical on religious matters, refusing the services of ministers, or any other Christian, for prayers when any member of the family was buried. They were a profane, Sabbath-breaking, rum-drinking family, of the toughest kind. They received me better than I expected ; but their best manners were rough enough to make me feel ill at ease. After hearing their rough talk for awhile I said to them, " I have come here to *recommend religion* and *pray* with you, if you are willing." I received this answer in substance, " Religion," said the old man ; " I like religion. My religion is to be clever and treat every body well ;" and then added, " I was asked a little while ago if I would treat the minister well if he called upon me, and I said, Why, yes ! I will give him all he wants to eat and to *drink* if he calls." " Well, then," said I, " be *clever* enough to let me talk and pray with you." He replied, " You may pray as much as you are a mind to, but it will never make the *corn grow !*" I then gave an exhortation on the subject nearest my heart, which I thought ap-

propriate for the time and place, without interruption, and then prayed. The men sat with
hats on their heads, and looked and listened
with apparent amazement. When I left I
thanked them for the privilege granted me.
The old man answered, "You are welcome to
all you have *got* by it, which isn't any thing.
If you will go to *planting corn* I will give you
some *seed*-corn," (the seed-corn was hanging in
the entry I was passing through.) I declined
the *seed-corn*, but told him I had got *just* what I
came for, namely, a talk *with* and prayer *for*
them, and then bade him and the family good-
bye. If no other result followed this dreaded
visit there was this : the old man would roundly
swear that "there was *one* minister who wasn't
ashamed nor *afraid* to come and see them !"
Many other hard spots in family visiting I
might name.

I will give but one more. In a certain town
in the south part of the conference I was making my first round of pastoral visits with one of
the class-leaders to pilot me and introduce me to
his members. We came to the house where one
of his class-members lived with her daughter,
whose husband was very irreligious, and when
in liquor very troublesome. It was in haying
time, and his work was in hearing distance of

the strange voices in the house. By invitation of the mother I prayed. He came in, greatly enraged, while we were at prayer, making a great noise with his feet and with the chairs. When prayer was ended, he roughly demanded, "*What does all this mean?*" All were silent for a time. Then I answered, "I am the pastor of the Church of which your mother-in-law is a member. I have come here for a pastoral call, and she invited me to pray, and I complied." He angrily answered, "No one has a right to command this house except myself!" I responded, "If I am an intruder I will leave." He showed me the door, and, with raised voice and fist, yelled out, "Clear out! *Clear out!* CLEAR OUT!" I left, calmly seeking the mercy of the Lord on his soul, and asking for grace to suffer for Christ's sake.

In my pastoral visits for many years past I have met with no such families, though I have sought to do a good amount of visiting, and I do not learn of similar annoyances (with extremely rare exceptions) in recent times. Our parishes being more compact, and our members and congregations nearer by, and denominational lines in the several charges being more distinctly known, our preachers generally visit their *own* people more exclusively, while the pastors of other Churches attend to *their* own without molestation.

The more faithful, impartial, and extensive the modern pastor in this department of labor now is, the more success he has with the people. He may do great good by going out among the neglected, the wandering, the vulgar and profane, and the neglecters of all churches, and invite them to church and to salvation.

The old and present disciplinary rule is, " Go into every house in course, and teach every one therein, young and old, to be Christians inwardly and outwardly ; make every particular plain to their understandings ; fix it in their minds ; write it on their hearts. In order to this, there must be line upon line, precept upon precept. What patience, what love, what knowledge is requisite for this !"* He cannot be an unfaithful pastor who will seek to live up to all such requirements.

CHAPTER VII.

Camp-Meetings Then and Now.

THESE meetings are of American, but not purely of Methodistic, origin. The first held in this country originated with and were sustained by the Presbyterians of the West, in connection with other denominations. The Methodists, however, soon became, more especially than others, their advocates and supporters.

Forty years ago they were common in all parts of the country where Methodism had sufficient numbers and influence to sustain them and appropriate places could be found for them. The preparation of the ground was a work demanding earnest and persevering effort on the part of both preachers and people living in the immediate vicinity where they were held.

It took days of hard work to cut up the brush, trim up the trees, level the ground, prepare the seats, and build the preachers' stand. Too often this work had to be performed by a few—the "burden-bearers" of the Church—and sometimes too much of it on the first day of the meeting.

Tents' companies, having at home prepared themselves as far as possible with cloth tents and cooked provisions, and secured means of conveyance in lumber-wagons, or more comfortable carriages, as convenience or necessity dictated, they started, the more distant ones on Monday morning, not much past "noon of night," for their annual "Feast of Tabernacles" in "the leafy grove."

The journey being performed, the happy but weary company immediately were busily at work leveling their tent-ground, cutting tent-poles, and putting up their tent; which, if accomplished in time, was followed by a good earnest prayer-meeting, and then "weary nature sought repose," which, however, under the new circumstances, was sometimes sought in vain. The next day the devotional exercises began in good earnest. Tents' companies, perhaps in all not more than twenty, had powerful prayer-meetings in their respective tents several times each day. Three or four sermons of special appropriateness and power were daily preached from the stand, and generally one public prayer-meeting also daily held.

Sinners were powerfully awakened, earnest seekers brought into the light and liberty of the Gospel, Christians quickened and specially blessed of the Lord, and shouts of victory were heard afar off. Thus the meeting went on, from day to day. The Friday evening prayer-meetings, by the consent of the presiding elder, were often held in the tents to a later hour than usually allowed. These were sometimes seasons of marvelous power. It was common at camp-meetings for some to be prostrated on the ground, overcome by what was called the " power of God." Skeptical "despisers beheld and wondered," while saints shouted aloud for joy.

The closing exercises, on Saturday morning, consisted of a brief address from the presiding . elder, or some one of the older preachers. Then a procession was formed, which marched around the ground, singing lustily good old Methodistic hymns to the familiar tunes of the day. · Then came the shaking-hand exercise with each and all in the procession. This parting scene was often very affecting. The word of hearty good cheer, the solemn "good-bye" with the prospect of meeting again in heaven if never again on earth, the tears of grief or joy, the shouts of praise, all rendered the scene deeply interesting, sometimes indescribably glorious. This done, then our tents were taken down, our goods loaded, and we were soon in our vehicles homeward bound, with "our hearts burning within us as Jesus talked with us by the way," and opened to us "new beauties in the King's highway of holiness."

What a change, in many important respects, in our camp-meeting arrangements and gatherings during the forty years past! Our camp-grounds are now owned, with few exceptions, by "camp-meeting associations," or leased for a series of years. They are well prepared, and furnished with a well-built preachers' stand and permanent seats, with pure water within easy reach, with boarding-houses for the multitude, and prices of fare reasonable. There are many permanent society tents, numerous family dwellings tolerably furnished, where some, yea many, are found in these pleasant homes for weeks in summer, before the regular camp-meeting begins, preferring such places to popular watering places or mountain rambles.

The mode of travel for the far off and nearer by, how changed! Instead of the slow team and lumber-wagon, we step into the rail-cars, and speed our way rapidly and easily to the ground. The needed preparations are quickly accomplished. Conveniences for self-boarding are such as to make the task comparatively light. The tents, society and family, are counted by hundreds, and the people in attendance by thousands. The mode of conducting the public and social exercises, from the changed circumstances of the meetings, are somewhat different from those in earlier times ; but the same "Master of assemblies" reveals himself, to sanctify, reclaim, convert, or quicken all the sincere worshipers. The modern camp-meeting, with all its financial improvements, increased accommodations, and real attractions, is now, as well as were those of earlier times, a divinely recognized means of grace, where vast numbers are yearly greatly quickened in the divine life, and "many added to the Lord of such as shall be saved."

These great camp-meeting centers also afford agreeable places for summer and healthful resort, in which to spend a few weeks away from the heat, bustle, and confusion of city life, and from country care and toil, without coming into disagreeable contact with all the demoralizing effects of degrading fashions in dress, social parties for sinful amusements, gambling and drinking dens, and disgusting flirtations, now disgracing all fashionable watering-places.

It is hoped that these camp-meeting centers may yet prove no small check to one of the most dangerous phases of modern society, as well as furnishing a great safeguard to the Church. Nevertheless, there is danger that our people shall become too lax in their tastes and habits, and allow objectionable amusements to be pressed into these now quiet and agreeable resorts while loitering there prior to the time for the gathering together of the great multitude for their annual " Feast of Tabernacles."

Against such dangers it is incumbent on our Church to keep her vigilant eye and her faithful sentinels, lest her "good be evil spoken of," Christ "wounded in the house of his friends," and God dishonored.

May the glory of this much-loved annual "feast," which from the first has been honored of the Lord by his special presence and saving power, become more and more glorious by being the spiritual birthplace of many thousands more!

CHAPTER VIII.

Parsonages and Churches.

THE METHODIST PARSONAGES THEN AND NOW.

THERE were few parsonages owned by the Methodist Episcopal Church forty years ago, and these were such as did not meet the real wants of the preacher's family. They were not conveniently arranged for family use, were generally small, cheap, and unpainted, and without carpets, sofas, or other furniture. Whatever commodities of this kind were enjoyed by the itinerant's family were generally brought from the last station, which was sometimes a distance of many miles, by team, and of course marred and bruised by the removal.

Sometimes two preachers were obliged, at great inconvenience and sacrifice, to occupy the same small parsonage. Where parsonages were not provided it was often very difficult to find·a home for the pastor's family. Some were fortunate enough to be able to hire houses for their own exclusive use, while others were obliged to take up with the scanty hired accommodations, at great inconvenience and discomfort, in houses with other occupants, often resulting in disagreeable·interruptions in many ways.

My memory runs back to the parsonage within the bounds of the circuit of my early home. It was a small, unpainted house, some two miles from the nearest place of Sabbath preaching, and without furniture except as provided by the occupants. In it lived both the circuit preachers of forty years ago. The circuit next to this in one direction had no parsonage. The pastor lived in a small, poorly finished, scantily furnished, old brown house, which must have been hired at small expense. The circuit next in another direction had a parsonage of fair size and appearance, with some better accommodations for the family comfort ; but this was a mile from church, and the pastor absent from home two thirds of the Sabbath at his other preaching-places, thus, from necessity, leaving his wife and children to get to and from church as best they could, or stay at home.

In other parts of New England the accommodations for ministers' homes might have been better than these, but extensive observation and general report confirm me in the belief that the foregoing represent an average of the homes of New England Methodist ministers forty years ago.

What favorable changes in these matters within the forty years past ! As Methodism has progressed in numbers and wealth, and as Churches have become more permanently gathered into centers of population and influence, the old circuits have been cut up into stations, and the result has been the erection or purchase of well-located, large, convenient, and somewhat expensive parsonages in most of our pastoral charges for the accommodation of our ministers. Some are respectably supplied by the societies with heavy furniture, carpets, etc., making them nearly ready for occupancy without burdensome effort on the part of the newly appointed pastor and family.

In some stations these accommodations are not found. The people of such stations see not yet their way clear to buy nor build ; but as a rule the stewards of these Churches seek to provide by rent suitable homes for their pastors. And whether parsonages are owned or houses hired by the proper officers of the Church, the good people of most of the stations have learned how to welcome their new pastors with both labor and money, and other substantial tokens without charge, thus cheering them in the sadness of removals and greatly lightening their burdens.

But with all these advantages now to be found in pastors' homes, in most of our stations, it is sad to know that there is yet a lack of either parsonages or hired houses in a few of our pastoral charges. Where no provision is made for them at the proper time extreme embarrassment and inconvenience are almost sure to follow, both to the pastor and to the people. These defects, it is hoped, will in time be remedied. The experience of the past should teach delinquents lessons of profit, and encourage the more thoughtful and prompt to perseverance in their labors of love.

Of the one hundred and fifteen stations in the New Hampshire Conference there are sixty-five parsonages reported, valued at a little more than $105,000. These embrace the good, bad, and indifferent, some ranging as high as $7,000, others as low as $500, or less. The average value is $1,600.* In the entire Methodist Episcopal Church in the United States there are between four and five thousand parsonages, with an estimated value of between seven and eight millions of dollars ; and they are being built on an average of four per week.

* New Hampshire Conference Minutes, 1872.

May the day soon come when each pastor's family in our Church shall be permitted to occupy a good, well-furnished parsonage !

OUR CHURCHES AND CHURCH ACCOMMODATIONS THEN AND NOW.

Forty years ago we had in different localities our Methodist chapels ; but they were generally without steeples, bells, belfries, paint, or cushioned pews, and rarely in any center of population, for there other more influential denominations held sway. But these chapels were more generally out in some retired school district, where the itinerants had preached and gathered converts till the place had become "too strait" for them, and, to meet the necessity, they would build a chapel. These places became centers of Methodist influence, whither the people of the Lord "went up to the testimony of Israel to give thanks unto the name of the Lord." In them our Methodistic fathers in the ministry in those days preached the word "in demonstration of the Spirit and of power." There were held our "old-fashioned quarterly meetings," when brethren and sisters came from the neighboring towns on Saturday, and tarried through all the services of Saturday and Sab-

bath ; and in some of them were held our annual
conferences. Besides these chapels we had, in
some instances,·our Sabbath services in what
were called union houses, and in meeting-houses
owned, but not occupied, by other denominations. But our places for public and social
worship, to a great extent, were school-houses,
dwelling-houses, and, in summer, even barns
and groves.

Such were our church accommodations, or I
might say want of accommodations, in most
parts of New England forty years ago. But
the good Lord was with his people then, and
" confirmed the word preached with signs following." Now only here and there an old-
fashioned chapel remains to remind us of the
past ; and we are happy to know that we have
almost entirely escaped from those entangling
alliances with other people caused by building
and occupying with them what have strangely
been termed " *union meeting-houses.*"

The Methodists have built and are building,
in the centers of influence and population, convenient, handsome, and sometimes costly churches,
·in which to worship God. Church-building
has been, with our people, a *specialty* for a few
years past. They were built in 1870 at the
rapid rate of over four for every working day in

the year.* We have now in the denomination, in this country, some fifteen thousand church edifices, worth nearly or quite $10,000,000, and affording sittings for more than four millions of people.

In the New Hampshire Conference, in 1872, there were reported in the Minutes one hundred and fifteen stations and one hundred and ten church edifices, valued at nearly $700,000, and, probably, affording sittings for forty thousand people. Some are but cheap and plain houses, while others were built at an expense of $60,000. It is believed that the rate of progress in church-building by the Methodists in this country is unparalleled by any other denomination of Christians in our land.

Modest and *free* churches at the first was our only usage, and is now our policy *as a Church*, however much we have departed from it in occasional instances. But *all Churches* are now beginning to look in that direction ; and it is believed that ultimately all our people will recognize it as a wise and just policy.

* Methodist Almanac, 1871

CHAPTER IX.

Opposition to Methodist Doctrines and Usages Forty Years Ago,* and Fraternal Relations of the Churches Now.

——◆——

INVALIDITY OF METHODIST ORDINATIONS.

FORTY years ago High Churchmen of England and America were bold and loud in proclaiming that John Wesley had no right to ordain Dr. Coke General Superintendent, or Bishop, of the Methodists in North America. They contended that there were *three distinct orders* in the ministry—bishop, elder, and deacon ; and that the *right of all ordinations* was vested in the bishop by virtue of an "unbroken succession" from the first · bishops—the apostles—and that if one link in the chain should be broken it would render invalid all succeeding ordinations ; and, therefore, as this chain was broken by Mr. Wesley, (he

* The writer acknowledges his indebtedness to Dr. N. Bangs' History of the Methodist Episcopal Church, vol. iv, for many of the facts of this chapter, and in some instances somewhat to his language, without the use of quotation marks.

being only an elder,) the Methodists had "*no Church, no ordained ministers, no sacraments.*" In a tract published and widely extended by them, called " Tracts for the People, No. IV," we find the following language : " Methodism is *not a Church—has no sacraments, has no ministry, no divine warrant.*" This is the general drift of the tract, and therefore we are prepared for its answer to its own question when it asks, " Well, if Methodism be not true, what has become of the thousands who have died in its connection ? *No reply is pretended! The human mind cannot tell that.* Let those who are living *see to themselves !* The salvation of your neighbor is not left to *you* to determine ; but it is left for *you* to be sure that *you* are in the way *most likely to save yourself.*" Though the doctrine of this tract had been proclaimed by High Churchmen from the first, yet this new attack, in this particular manner, created much bitter feeling and strife. It was answered in an able manner in a tract (No. 305) by Dr. George Peck.

Similar attacks were made by others on our Church polity, but able writers were raised up "in defense of our fathers." Among other works, Dr. N. Bangs' book on " An Original Church of Christ " came to our defense. He

took the position that the doctrine of uninter-
rupted succession from the apostles in a *third
order* by a *triple* consecration, as distinct from
and superior to presbyters, has been discarded
by most ecclesiastical writers as resting on no
solid foundation, not being susceptible of proof
from any authentic source ; that the word of
God and the testimonies of the primitive fathers
of the Church went to sustain the idea that
bishops and presbyters were the *same order*,
though different offices, and that Mr. Wesley,
in providing for his spiritual children, invaded
no man's right, nor assumed that which did not
belong to him. This was the position of our
Church, and most of her ministers and members became pretty thoroughly posted on the
subject. Our bishops, we claim, are in the true
"apostolic succession."

OPPOSITION TO METHODIST DOCTRINE.

Calvinists then strenuously opposed our
Methodistic doctrines of " Free Grace," " Free
Will," " The Witness of the Spirit of our Adoption," and " Danger of Apostasy ;" but they
gloried in " Divine Sovereignty," " Fore-ordina-
tion," in election of some from all eternity to
eternal life, "and reprobation of others to damnation," and the impossibility of apostasy from

true conversion." These opposing views created·
much discussion. Our views were stoutly de-
fended by Dr. W. Fisk in a work called "Calvinistic Controversy," and by our preachers
generally. They were "bold in our God" to
defend the true "Gospel with much contention."

The young reader may be assisted in forming
some clearer idea than he otherwise could of the
outspoken Calvinism of those days by the following interesting reminiscences :

On one of my early circuits a good deacon of
a certain Church of the Calvinistic faith related
to me, with deep emotion, his Christian experience in substance as follows : "Away back
many years ago," said he, "the Spirit of the
Lord sought me out, and opened my heart.
The law then entered 'and slew me,' and
pushed me to the very verge of hell. The
more the Spirit showed me my wicked heart,
and the nearer I came to the verge of hell, (till
I thought every moment I should drop in,) the
more I *hated* God, and most gladly would I
have dethroned him if I had the power. I
hated him with *perfect hatred*. At that *very
moment* Jesus Christ came and took me into
his *loving arms*." "By faith," I responded.
"No," said the good old man, "there was not

a *jot of faith about it*, till my rebellious heart
was changed from nature to grace. Then I had
faith *given* me, and I *repented*, but not before."
Not far from this time I heard his minister
preach, who was also a Calvinist of "the strait-
est sort." The time and circumstances, which
no doubt called out the sermon, were peculiar,
and need explanation.

My Sabbath appointment in one part of my
circuit came where the Methodists had no
church edifice, and the Church of the Calvinistic faith had one, which they occupied only
each alternate Sabbath. They therefore kindly
offered its use to the Methodists for the other
Sabbaths, which was gladly accepted. I had
taken occasion to preach on a certain Sabbath
on "the higher Christian life," and "the danger
of final apostasy," to the great annoyance, as I
afterward found, of my Calvinistic hearers.

The week following the denomination owning
the church held a "ministerial association"
therein, which I attended. The old pastor had
never seen me before, but had heard of my *het-
erodoxical* sermon, as he regarded it. When
about to commence his services he turned to a
ministerial associate, and pointing down in the
direction where I was sitting, asked, as I thought,
" Isn't that the young Methodist preacher who

preached here last Sabbath?" and in response received a nod of "yes." When commencing his sermon he in effect said, "I am peculiarly impressed to take the following text: 'We are his workmanship, created in Christ Jesus unto good works, which God hath before ordained, that we should walk in them.'" Ephes. ii, 10. He explained it thus: "The metaphor of the text is one which relates to the erection of a building. The *marksman* goes out into the forest and *selects* the trees he would use in the erection of his building; so the Holy Spirit goes out and *selects* his favorite subject, and *marks* him as his own by opening his heart. Then comes the *axman* and *fells* the tree which has been thus marked; so the law of God enters the *marked* sinner, whose heart has been opened to receive it, and '*slays* him.' Then comes the *hewer* and scores and hews and straightens out the timber; but, *mind you*, he leaves *all the old heart in.* So the Gospel comes in and *straightens out* the crooked ways of the *selected* sinner—smooths off the *rough spots*, and cuts off the *knots*, and thus prepares him for a place in the 'spiritual temple.' But, *mind you*," said he, with peculiar emphasis and gesture, "he leaves all the *old heart in him.* Perfection is perfection, and it doesn't belong to man. Do *you* think any body can be perfect with *all the old heart left in him?* No such thing. Then the timber is taken to the place for the erection of the building, and *framed* into it, and *pinned in.* And do *you* think it can get out again? I tell you no. Jesus Christ has said, 'None shall *pluck* them out of my hands, and my Father is greater than I, and no man shall be able to *pluck* them out of my Father's hands ; and *they shall never perish.'"* This he said with a peculiarly triumphant gusto. Thus, according to his plan, the great "spiritual temple" of the Lord was being built by God's *sovereign* and *electing* grace.

At the noon recess he sought an introduction to me, and invited me to preach the afternoon sermon, saying, " They have heard *one side* this morning, let them have *the other side* this afternoon." I thought it a strange request, and feared he sought a quarrel on doctrinal matters. Young as I was I dreaded to preach under such circumstances, and delayed to answer till I had consulted some of my own Church-members present. By their advice I consented, and preached on " the *other side," the Methodist side.* My subject was that of "a living, active faith, and its experimental and practical fruits." The Lord graciously helped me to preach a warm and earnest sermon. The old Calvinist pastor and others followed with strong indorsements of the sermon, and with warm exhortations. The forenoon sermon was not made the theme of the afternoon, as some hoped and others feared. The people saw that "the *other*," the *Methodist*, "side" was a contention for a religion "which is first *pure*, then *peaceable*, without *partiality*, and without hypocrisy, full of mercy and *good fruits.*" Such old Calvinistic ideas are now seldom repeated either by the modern press or pulpit, though still the comparatively silent belief of some.

OPPOSITION TO METHODIST CHURCH POLITY— SECESSIONS.

Severe attacks were often made upon our Church government forty years ago. Secessions from the Church had already taken place, resulting in the organization of the "Reformed Methodist Church" and of the "Protestant Methodist Church." These seceders were with us in doctrine, but very strenuously opposed to our episcopacy and Church government, especially our lack of the lay element, in our Annual and General Conferences. The misnamed "Boston Olive Branch" employed pens dipped "in the bitterest gall," and sent out its weekly slanders. "The History and Mystery of Methodist Episcopacy," by one Alexander McCaine—a scurrilous attack upon our Church —was freely circulated. Dr. Thomas E. Bond, an able writer, and others wrote much in our defense. Dr. John Emory, afterward Bishop, came out with the "Defense of Our Fathers," against the unjust accusations of McCaine. These controversies, though occurring in 1827 and 1828, had their influence forty years ago, and Bishop Emory's "Defense" was republished in 1835. The Church, in those days, stood strong against any innovation of her polity. The time had not then come for a favorable verdict for lay representation.

OPPOSITION TO OUR SUNDAY-SCHOOL, BIBLE, AND
 TRACT SOCIETY—ORGANIZATIONS SEPARATE
 FROM THE AMERICAN SOCIETY, SO CALLED.

The organization of the "Methodist Sunday-School Society," separate from the "American," rendered it necessary for our people to supply our own schools with suitable books from the Methodist press. But, as Bibles and Testaments were published by the "American Bible Society," professedly for all denominations alike, the "Methodist Episcopal Church" asked the "Young Men's Bible Society of New York," constituted *expressly* to.supply needy Sunday-schools gratuitously, to supply the Methodist schools as they did others. The request was rejected on the plea that *ours* were sectarian schools! This rendered it necessary, in order to supply our schools with the word of life, to organize the " Bible Society of the Methodist Episcopal Church," which being done created no little opposition from various quarters.

Methodist literature, which up to this time had been considered in the background, was now brought into public notice by the publication of the "Christian Advocate," and the issue from our Book Room of " Wesley's Sermons," " Clarke's Commentaries," " The Methodist Magazine," and numerous Tracts of a doctrinal, practical, and experimental character, and by the continual augmentation of books on a variety of subjects, together with the increasing prosperity of Methodist missions, which seemed to awaken the attention of others, and to call forth strictures upon our doctrines and general economy of such a character as to call for self-defense.

There seemed to have been a combined effort on the part of other sects to destroy, if possible, the influence of Methodism. Calvinistic editors in different parts of the country, almost simultaneously, uttered the same language against this rising people, without mitigating their severity by acknowledging even any good accomplished by them.

Dr. Adam Clarke was accused of introducing into his " Commentary " "unauthorized criticisms upon the original text." Wesley was accused in his "Notes on the New Testament" of mutilating the sacred text in such a manner as to make " nonsense of the plainest texts in the Bible." These foolish accusations, though severe, were such as the books themselves, by being critically and candidly read, would annihilate. *Methodist ministers' characters* were ungenerously assailed, by calling in question their integrity.

It was stated in some quarters that Methodism had an *immense fund* at her command, by which her ministers were supported independently of the people ; and that these funds were so dexterously managed that the Methodist people themselves did not know either their extent or application, they being kept in ignorance by "cunningly devised artifices."

This accusation was promptly met by facts. It was demonstrated that all the profits derived from the " Book Concern " and the "Chartered Fund"—the only funds of the Church—did not yield over *three dollars* a year to each claimant; and that the superannuated and supernumerary preachers, and the widows and orphans of preachers, who were the legal claimants of these funds, did not receive—including all voluntary contributions—over twenty-five, fifty, or seventy-five per cent. of their " Disciplinary Claims," which was one hundred dollars for such preacher or widow, and not over twenty-four dollars per year for each dependent child.

Another complaint brought against the Methodists was their manner of holding Church property. It was alleged that it was deeded to the General Conference, and that the Methodist laity had no control of it. To this it was replied, that the statement was false at every point ; that instead of being secured to the *conference*, and therefore the property of the *preachers*, it was held by *trustees* appointed by the *people*, where the laws of the States in which it was located provided for that manner of appointment, and in other places as the Discipline directed, that is, by trustees, for the *use* of the members of the Methodist Episcopal Church in that place.

It was claimed by our opponents that our Church government was not only unscriptural, but set up and vindicated in "*contempt of script-*

ure authority." ' This led to a scriptural defense of our .Church government, our itinerancy, and general method of conducting affairs, by various able Methodist writers.

"AMERICAN HOME MISSIONS" AND THE "MISSISSIPPI VALLEY."

The controversy in regard to the "American Home Missionary Society" and the "*moral destitution*" of the West, and especially that of the "Great Mississippi Valley," was still agitating the public mind, though it had been the "bone of contention" from the year 1826, when the said society was organized by the union of the "Presbyterian," "Dutch Reformed," and "Congregationalist" Churches, with the avowed intention of filling up the "waste places of Zion," and establishing Churches which should adopt the Church polity of either denomination, in accordance with the preferences of the people composing the Church thus gathered. Their agents had been, and were then, going among *all the people* to whom they could gain access, and gathering funds to promote its objects. Its patrons gave it the name of the "*National Society.*" The people were misguided by this appellation, as it was far from embracing *all evangelical Christian Churches,* or even a majority of them. The Methodists and the Baptists were not included, though each were more numerous than either of the aforesaid denominations. The " Episcopalians," the " Lutherans," and several other denominations, were not embraced in it, and yet it was called "*national.*" To this the Methodists properly uttered their decided protest. More than this, " the *moral wastes* of the Valley of the Mississippi " were so *fearfully* reported by agents and official reporters, and such alarming descriptions of those sections were given; as greatly excited the friends of Christianity. Thrilling notes of complaint were echoed from one end of the continent to the other about the " uneducated ministers," "incompetent ministers," and so on, of that great valley, and the people, in strains of mournful eloquence, appealed to for aid in such earnestness as to give great alarm. Said Dr. Lyman Beecher, the father of the Beechers, " The nation must arise and save itself by its own energies. The trumpet must sound *long* and *loud;* the press must *groan,* and utter in the ears of our countrymen the story of their miseries, or the nation is undone." This note of alarm, sounded by Dr. Beecher, continned to roll through the whole country, until the doleful

ditty of the "*moral destitution* of the great valley " reverberated from hill to valley with sick-
ening repetition.

Now, what were the facts pertaining to that
same "*moral waste?*" At the very time when
these alarms were sounding through the length
and breadth of our land various denominations
of evangelical Christians had good and prosperous Churches there. Our own Church at that
very time, had seven annual conferences in the
valley, between five and six hundred traveling
preachers, and twice this number of local
preachers ; and her Church-membership there
was more than one hundred and thirty thousand.

That there was a call for additional aid there
can be no reasonable doubt ; but to call other ministers than their own " *incompetent,*" "*uneducated,*" or " *inefficient,*" was, to say the least, not agreeable to those thus dishonored. Indeed, in many
of these reports there seemed to be an effort to
depreciate those who had labored long and successfully in those parts represented as " moral
wastes."

The Methodist Church, very properly, resented
these unjust representations, and in her own
official organ, the " Christian Advocate," succeeded in a few years, by an honest exhibit of
facts, in disabusing the public mind to a great

extent on the subject; but its influence was felt for many years after.

We often heard that old echo, "The great moral waste!" "The moral destitution of the Mississippi Valley!" "Uneducated and incompetent ministers!" The facts which were elicited by this state of things, of the numerical strength of Methodism in that great valley and elsewhere, were creditable to *our Church*, but damaging to the *official agents* and *reporters* of the "American Home Missionary Society."

THE TEMPERANCE QUESTION.

The American Temperance Society forty years ago was doing much good—exerting a powerful influence on the bodies and souls of our countrymen. It had been in active operation since 1826. Our Church at first took a position, through her official organ and many of her leading men, which was somewhat antagonistic to the American Society in some of its measures, though intending to advocate the practice of abstinence in her membership, her stringent General Rules requiring that they shall avoid evil of every kind, and prohibiting especially "drunkenness, buying or selling spirituous liquors, or *drinking them*, unless in cases of necessity." Our position on the subject·being misunderstood, no little uneasiness was created and much earnest discussion elicited. The Methodists took the ground that this general rule of our Church already made our people members of a total abstinence society, and that to come into the measures of the American Society would be a virtual acknowledgment that our Church, as such, needed to be reformed.

Another objection to the American Society was, that it proposed to raise the sum of $20,000 as a *permanent fund* for the support of an agent or agents, who should be exclusively devoted to the temperance cause ; which proposition our people did not think expedient, preferring the plan of raising the money for necessary expenses when it should be needed.

This position created some heart-burnings on both sides, and elicited no little discussion ; but it brought to light facts which had been concealed before. Though unchanged in regard to the financial policy of the American Society, it was found that the *stringent* rule of the Discipline of the Church had been so *softened* down in the minds of some that it had (in their view) become a dead-letter, and that they were in the habitual daily practice of *drinking*, and others of *selling*, intoxicating liquors, as was

then too commonly practiced by other professed
Christians. This led to important results. Our
people saw the necessity of temperance pledges
and of temperance societies, and (to the great
profit and edification of the Church and the
cause of God generally) entered into the work
and measures of the temperance cause.

This reference here made to the financial
plan for *permanent* funds and *paid* agents of the
society, and Methodist opposition thereto, re-
minds me of the strife created on this ground
forty years ago on the first circuit I traveled
after joining conference. In our temperance
efforts of that year some proposed to our people
to join in the cause on the plan of the American
Society's financial polity. Though our people
were as earnest advocates of total abstinence
as any others, yet our preacher in charge and
many of his members strenuously opposed the
measure. This resulted in the formation of
two distinct societies—one auxiliary to the
American, and the other an independent one—
and between the two there was but little fellowship or co-operation.

Such controversies and strifes, however, in a
few years passed away, and all the friends of
the cause entered heartily into this much-needed
reform with great unanimity. Our Methodist

people are now, and for the past twenty years and more have been, the vanguard in the great temperance army. These are some of the controversies which Methodism had to grapple with, coming from outside influences, in days gone by, of which many of our youthful readers have had but little knowledge.

Other false theories were common in those days, but they were not directed against our doctrines and usages more than against other evangelical Churches. Among these were Universalism and open infidelity. These fallacious and soul-destroying sentiments were perhaps about equally opposed by all evangelical Churches. These old heresies have now taken other forms of error, and appear under the name " Free Religion," the elastic bands of which are so extended as to take in what are called " Liberal Christianity," " Spiritualism," " Free-lovism," " Free Thinkers," and so on.

The old Calvinistic ideas, if held at all, are now resting in the shade, seldom advocated in public or elsewhere in the light of day. "Apostolic succession " and its consequent claims, though still the faith of most Churchmen, are not now in the way of our progress, our people having ceased to feel the force of their attacks against our doctrines and usages,

Lay Representation has now become the policy of our Church. Seceders from her have mainly laid down their weapons of warfare. The American Bible Society is now equally ours with all other Christian denominations, and receives our hearty support. God is with us, leading this "sacramental host" on to certain victory. May nothing transpire to dampen the prospect!

CONTROVERSIES ON UNIVERSALISM—ANECDOTES.

The writer has referred to the popular theory of universal salvation, which once had extensive influence in our country. Our ministers had to meet this doctrine in those days, perhaps, more frequently than preachers of other denominations, inasmuch as their itinerant system brought them oftener into such contact. The young reader may be aided in his estimate of some of the controversies of those days by the following anecdotes, which we will here record, more for the shrewdness of some of our older preachers than for their modesty or politeness.

On my first circuit, after joining conference, the following story was often repeated. A certain Universalist minister of note had by previous appointment brought together a large audience to hear his arguments against the doctrine of the endless punishment of the wicked. Among others several Methodist ministers attended, one of whom was the eccentric, blunt, but talented Rev. J. W. Hardy, presiding elder of the district. The Universalist, in a flowery and flippant manner, but with shallow arguments, sought to annihilate all the arguments of opponents of his doctrine. When through he said, "I perceive there are several clergymen present. I shall be pleased to hear them speak on the subject I have presented." All refused but Father Hardy, who began in his peculiar manner of voice and gestures, more easily imitated than transferred to paper with pen and ink, and tore the arguments of the sermon into shreds, to the great chagrin of some, and the equal satisfaction of others.

Then the first speaker again arose and said, "The arguments of the gentleman who has just addressed you are not relevant to the subject. He has not touched my main points of argument, and I hope that the people will not be influenced by what the reverend speaker has said."

Father Hardy was soon again on his feet, and related this cutting story : "A certain old negro was walking the highway one day, and passing a flock of geese, the *old gander* got up and stuck out his neck, and running after him, quacked and *quacked* at him. The negro *caught* him, and *wrung* his neck for him, and threw him down in a *mud-puddle;* and what did the old gander do but jump up again, and, sticking out his bill, again quacked out, ' I've beat, I've beat, I've beat.' ". The effect on the audience can be better imagined than described. The story has often been repeated for these past forty years in that town and all the regions round about, and will be doubtless handed down to posterity by those it pleases, and by some who condemn its uncouthness.

Universalists of those days had a great deal to say against the idea of a "personal devil," and our preachers often came in contact with this sentiment, and had a short-hand method of disposing of their arguments. Illustration : When on my first circuit, after joining conference, I went with my preacher in charge to the Universalist minister, a man in high repute among his own people, and invited him to join with us in a certain Christian benevolent enterprise in town. He objected on account of our difference in doctrinal points, and named in particular the belief of Methodists and other orthodox people in the personality of the devil. The Methodist replied, " The Saviour himself was tempted by the devil." To which the Universalist responded, "There is no devil but human nature to tempt people, and Christ was tempted by his own nature." "Then," said the Methodist preacher, "you believe Christ had the devil in him, do you?" He answered in substance, "He possessed a human nature, and was tempted by it." Said the other, "I think I understand you, then, that Christ had the devil in him." His reply was, "If you report me I do not want to be reported in that light." "Very well," said the Methodist, "I shall be glad to hear you make any explanation which will relieve you." He undertook it, but with no satisfaction to us or relief to himself. The interview ended by the reply of the brother Methodist : "It is all plain, I see, that you say our blessed Saviour had the devil in him." We soon parted, but our clerical friend didn't seem to enjoy his mind very well.

FRATERNAL RELATIONS OF THE METHODIST EPISCOPAL CHURCH WITH OTHER EVANGELICAL CHURCHES.

Methodism began in America under one organization. This unity continued only from 1766, when Philip Embury formed the first class in New York city, which consisted of five members, to the year 1792, when James O'Kelley, a popular preacher in Virginia, led off by secession a portion of the Church, and formed what was called "The Republican Methodist Church," afterward called "The Christian Church." *

Other secessions occurred from time to time from various causes, resulting in separate Church organizations, so that in 1832 there were "The Reformed Methodist Church," "The Protestant Methodist Church," "The African Methodist Episcopal Church," "The African Methodist Episcopal Zion Church," "The Canada Wesleyan Methodist" and "Canada Episcopal Methodist" Churches. In none of these organizations were there any doctrinal differences. But differences arose on Church polity, causing serious alienations among the so-called "O'Kelley party," the Reformers, and the Methodist Protestants. The prejudice against color, and the alienations caused thereby, produced the "African Methodist" organizations ; and the separation by the national boundary line the Canadian organizations. Though these separate organizations, taken separately or collectively, were small compared with the Parent Church,

* See Bangs' History of the Methodist Episcopal Church.

yet there was a break in the unity of Methodism in America which was deeply regretted by
most lovers of true Church harmony. With
some of these Churches there was no official
reciprocal connection.

Our General Conference held only fraternal
relations, *officially*, with the " English Wesleyan
Methodist Conference." They sent their " Fraternal Delegates " to us, and, in return, our Conference sent ours to them, who on either side
were most cordially received and honorably
treated.

Denominational Churches of other names,
and of opposite doctrinal views as well as polity, held nó official cordial relations with our
Church. Old doctrinal controversies, misrep-
resentations of our doctrines and usages by our
enemies, and sectarian jealousies, kept them
from any hearty and friendly co-operation with
the Methodist denomination.

How different the fraternal unity manifested
in the General Conference of 1872 ! Fraternal
delegates came to this ecclesiastical council of
our Church from " The English Wesleyan,"
" The Wesleyan Irish," " The Wesleyan Methodist " of Canada, " The Methodist Episcopal
Canadian," " The Wesleyan Methodist East
British," " The Protestant Methodist," " The

Methodist Church" Conferences, and "The Evangelical German" Methodist "Association."

In addition to these representatives from these various branches of Methodist Churches of various names, there were fraternal delegates from "The Presbyterian General Assembly," "The Congregational Church," various "Baptist Churches," "The Free Church of Italy," and from several other religious bodies, each extending to our Church the right-hand of fellowship.

Their hearty reception by the General Conference, their words of congratulation, the friendly salutations they brought from the different Churches they represented, the responses given to them, and the appointment of "Fraternal Delegates" by the Conference to extend our friendly greeting in return, all show the progress which is being made toward the much-to-be-desired Christian unity of the Churches. Even preliminary plans were made by our Church in that Conference for a friendly correspondence with the alienated Methodist Episcopal Church South, and the prospect has never appeared better for the unification of American Methodism since the different separations occurred than at this time. .

Old prejudices are melting away. The different Church organizations of evangelical Prot-

estantism are learning to embrace each other ·
with unity in the essentials of Christianity, with
liberty to differ in non-essentials, and in all
things to exercise that " charity which is the
bond of perfectness."

CHAPTER X.

Woman's Work in the Methodist Episcopal Church Forty Years Ago and Now.

ETHODISM, from its origin, has given to woman a sphere of Christian effort and influence superior to any other Church organization since the days of primitive Christianity, and has continued to open new fields to her for the use of her Christian capabilities as few Churches now afford or venture to allow.

Heathenism has ever degraded woman ; but Christianity, " pure and undefiled," has ever exalted her, mentally, socially, and morally. But by misinterpretation of those Scriptures which refer to her sphere in the Church, and too much after the manner of heathen nations, she has been placed far below the level of " the lords of creation " in regard to her right of public oral testimony for her Lord and Master. Her lips have been sealed from such testimony in the presence of men.

Methodism has opened her once sealed lips and bade her voice be heard in living testimonies of Christ, and employed her capabilities in various appropriate missions of mercy and love. We remember having heard her voice in prayer and exhortation in our youthful days.

Forty years ago she was always heard in our social meetings. Often in our public assemblies she bore her faithful testimony for her Lord. Though seldom did she stand in " the sacred desk," yet in various ways, like the Marys of old, did she proclaim to the people a crucified and risen Saviour.

Since then woman's sphere of influence has been increasing, and new fields of usefulness for her have been multiplying. Old prejudices have been dying out among other religious sects, so that in some churches, where once her voice was silenced, she has now the privilege of being Christ's oral witness to the people of his saving grace.

Among Methodists she receives a cordial welcome, when fitted " by gifts, grace, and usefulness," into our pulpits as a helper in the Gospel ministry. She finds appropriate work at our altars in pleading with God for immortal souls, and on the platform in earnest pleadings with the people for their co-operation in the various great enterprises of Christian benevolence in which the Church is enlisted. She finds some of these new openings brought into organic form, where she is more *specially* recognized, socially and officially. Among these are "The Ladies' and Pastors' Christian Union," and "The Woman's Foreign Missionary Society."

The recent General Conference has, officially, uttered the voice of Methodism in the following

REPORT OF THE COMMITTEE ON "WOMAN'S WORK
IN THE CHURCH."

"Your Committee have had before them several papers on the work of women in the Church. The subject which these papers present are such as the licensing and ordaining of women as preachers, 'The Ladies' and Pastors' Christian Union,' 'The Woman's Foreign Missionary Society,' and propositions for the enlargement of Christian and benevolent activity.

"We can but rejoice in these manifestations of increasing interest on the part of women in all that pertains to the activity of the Church, and are devoutly thankful for this fresh awakening of zeal for Christian work.

"It has ever been characteristic of Methodism to welcome to the Church all available agencies for carrying forward the Redeemer's kingdom, and for the salvation of souls. From the beginning, also, the Methodist Church has recognized and used the peculiar capabilities of women ; in every period of our history women have been active counselors with men in the service of the Church, and in not a few instances have been recognized leaders in important movements. Many names of Christian heroines adorn the pages of our Church history.

" These recent manifestations of a desire for activity for Christ are not a novelty, but a revival of the true spirit of Methodism, in which we greatly rejoice, and from ·which we expect the most happy results. More than two thirds of the members of the Church are women. That they have a place and a work in the Church is not doubted, but to define and designate the exact character and fields of their labor is not an easy matter.

" In this as in most other interests of the Church important questions are gradually settling themselves, and Providence is itself pointing out large and important fields which can be most efficiently occupied by women, and into which we find the noblest spirits are vigorously entering. Our women are already far on toward leading the advance in the actual work of the Sabbath-school, our Home and City Missions, in the distribution of tracts, and in the visitation of the poor and neglected masses.

"Recently God has directed their hearts toward their sisters of foreign countries, and a most successful organization has been effected for aiding in the evangelization of heathen lands. For these fields of labor they have peculiar capabilities, and we rejoice that the Divine Spirit is leading their hearts earnestly into them.

"In regard to woman's preaching, we must wait the further developments of Providence. We rejoice in indications that women are called to be teachers of the Word of Life, and yet the instances are not sufficiently numerous to justify any new legislation in the Church on this subject.

"We commend the 'Woman's Foreign Missionary Society' and 'The Ladies' and Pastors' Christian Union' as two organizations worthy of the highest gifts and noblest efforts. We exhort the women of the Church to still greater zeal in the Sunday-school, the class-room, the prayer-meetings, and the love-feasts, and in the evangelization of the masses.

"We exhort our preachers also to give all
wise, discreet encouragement they can to the
exercise and development of the gifts which
God has bestowed on our sisters for the further-
ance of his kingdom on the earth."

Such are the new organic spheres now open
for her usefulness in our Church, which man
cannot as successfully occupy. She can go to
the poor and needy with her messages of mercy—to the degraded of her sex with her gentle
pleadings for reform—to the despised and neglected with the words of encouragement and
deeds of kindness—and to lands of heathen
darkness, where woman is down-trodden and
degraded, and find access to those of her sex
from whom our male missionaries are utterly
excluded, and teach her the way to heaven.

Great as may be the sacrifices and imminent
the perils of her mission, her faith and heroism
are equal to the demand. Under the all-sus-
taining power and exalting influences of grace,
she shall be more than conqueror. At home,
she can employ her social influence, her voice
and pen in pleading with and for her sex that
the glorious Gospel, which is free for all, and
can "save to the uttermost all who come unto
him," may become to all her kind "a savor of

life unto life." Such sacrifices and offerings, with her fervent prayers of faith, will prove as pleasing to her Lord as did the "precious ointment" poured upon his head by the humble Mary of old, and her noble deeds shall be "spoken of as a memorial of her wherever the Gospel shall be preached."

CHAPTER XI.

Methodism and Sunday-Schools.

———•———

UNDAY-SCHOOLS forty years ago, compared with our numerical strength as a Church, were quite numerous among our people, and many of them were very prosperous. They were sustained in nearly each of the places where we had Sabbath preaching. Even where we had no church edifices, and were obliged to worship on the Sabbath in school-houses, or in public halls, we had our organized Sunday-schools in somewhat successful operation, especially in the more favorable seasons of the year.

While Sunday-schools were thus making a deep impression on the public religious mind, nearly all denominations adopted them, none more eagerly than did the Methodist Episcopal Church. Definite forms of conference reports were made out, and accurate statistics of their numbers and state in each pastoral charge were reported to conference, embracing the number of officers, teachers, and scholars. The sum total of officers, teachers, and scholars reported in the General Minutes of the Church forty years ago was not less than one hundred thousand.

Methodism had recognized and encouraged Sunday-schools from their very origin. Wesley saw that those first established, by Robert Raikes, were of God. Some of the female members of his Societies were the first to offer *gratuitous instruction* in them. In America, as early as the year 1786, Bishop Asbury founded a Sunday-school in Virginia. "This first school in America" prefigured one of the most important later advantages of the institution, by giving to the Methodist Episcopal Church a useful minister of the Gospel.*

* For a more detailed account of the early progress and origin of Sunday-schools, see the "Report of the Sunday-School Union for 1851."

It is a singular fact that, with all the records of the origin of Sunday-schools in America, there should still be such tardiness among other denominations of Christians in recognizing their Methodistic origin.

It has been claimed in some quarters that Bishop White, of the Episcopal Church, organized the "first in America" which had any permanency. This was in Philadelphia, in 1791. But this was five years after Bishop Asbury's school in Virginia. A recent writer in the "New York Evangelist" reports that a Sunday-school was organized in what is now the city of Pittsburgh, Pa., in the year 1809, and claims it as

The Methodist Episcopal Church was the
first to put Sunday-schools into organic relation to her Conference Minutes. This was done

the "first," in these words: "I mention this fact," says he,
"that the origin of Sunday-schools, in their history, may be
properly recorded in the United States." Another writer re-
cently, through the "Boston Daily News," claims that "the
Puritans originated" the "first Sunday-school in America, in
Roxbury, Mass., in 1674." Also, "that Ludwig Thacker anticipated Robert Raikes by establishing a Sunday-school in
Ephrath, Pa., in the year 1750, which continued thirty years."
A reliable answer to these statements will be found in the
following extract from a letter to the writer, by Daniel Wise,
D.D., one of the best-posted writers on Sunday-schools in
America, he having been for sixteen years past the editor of
the "Sunday-School Advocate," also of the Sunday-School
Union Library Books, and a voluminous writer on the subject
of Sunday-schools. He says: "There can be no room for
reasonable doubt respecting the introduction of Sunday-schools
of modern times into America by Bishop Asbury, in 1786.
That sporadic cases of Sunday instruction occurred before that
period is probable. Such cases were known in Europe before
Mr. Raikes' school, but they did not grow into a system like
his. Mr. Asbury, doubtless, brought the modern Sunday-school
idea from England, and gave it practical form in America, long
before any other person or Church thought of doing so. The
sporadic cases mentioned do not set aside his claim, for they
never grew. They were purely local, limited, and died seedless.
His schools spread, lived, were recognized by the Methodist
Episcopal Church, and finally became one of her organic parts.
You may fearlessly challenge the 'Daily News' writers to produce an analogous case, and defy them to rob our Church of
the historic honor of founding the American Sunday system."
Such errors as Dr. Wise has here corrected concerning the
origin of Sunday-schools in America surprised some of us

as early as 1790, at the conference held in Charleston, S. C., Bishop Asbury presiding. This conference voted to establish Sunday-schools "for poor children, white and black." In 1827 the Sunday-School Union was organized. In 1828 the General Conference made it the duty of presiding elders to promote Sunday-schools in their districts, and preachers in charge to report Sunday-school statistics.

Such a lively interest had Methodists taken in Sunday-schools all through their early history that it will not be a matter of special wonder that the cause was found to be in this encouraging state forty years ago ; yet there were many defects in their practical workings which could not be remedied except by more experience, and by wisely-directed and prayerful, persevering efforts, such as time and needs should develop.

They were not as thoroughly organized as efficiency required. They were too frequently suspended in the winter. They were deficient

who had made ourselves somewhat familiar with what we regarded as the authentic history of Sunday-schools in our country, and what we had supposed were the acknowledged facts by all well-read men on the subject. Query: Is it sectarian prejudice which causes people to withhold from our Methodistic fathers the credit of founding Sabbath-schools in America ?

in the number and variety of suitable library
books, especially for juveniles. They were
without the needed "Sunday-School Requisites."
They had no Sunday-school periodicals. With
all these drawbacks there was but a limited opportunity to develop what Sunday-schools could
with better facilities accomplish. Nevertheless
the cause gained volume and power constantly.

In 1840 Sunday-schools in our pastoral
charges were placed under the control of the
quarterly conferences. In 1841 the "Sabbath-
School Messenger" was started, and for eight
years was published in Boston. Then the
"Sunday-School Advocate" was established in
New York, and the "Messenger" merged into
it. In 1844 the Rev. D. P. Kidder, D.D., was
elected editor of the "Sunday-School Advocate"
and of the Sunday-school library books, and Secretary of the "Sunday-School Union," in which
capacity he served till 1856, when the Rev. D.
Wise, D.D., became, by the appointment of the
General Conference, his successor in office,
which he held till 1872. In 1868 Rev. J. H.
Vincent, D.D., was appointed editor of the
newly-authorized "Sunday-School Teachers'
Journal," and of "Sunday-School Requisites."
The General Conference of 1872 elected him
editor of "Sunday-School Books," the "Sun-

day-School Advocate," the "Sunday-School Journal," and "Sunday-School Requisites."

Thus it appears that from the first our progress has been constant and rapid, but particularly so for the past forty years. We now number not less than 1,500,000 members, including officers and teachers ; 2,000 volumes of Sunday-school books are published by the Sunday-School Union ; nearly 400,000 copies of the "Sunday-School Advocate," exclusive of the Canada edition, are circulated ; the "Sunday-School Journal" has more than 70,000 subscribers ; the yearly conversions to Christ in our Sunday-schools are reported to number some 40,000 or 50,000, while the "Department of Sunday-School Requisites" is the most extensive and complete of its kind in the entire country.

"The Berean Series of Lessons," edited by Dr. Vincent, is an important feature of improvement in the mode of instruction ; and the "Lesson Leaves," freshly taken from the word of God, the only "tree of life," whose leaves are for the "healing of the nations," are found in many, and should be in all, our Sunday-schools.

The "Sunday-School Journal," for superintendents, teachers, and adult scholars, is crowded full of the freshest and best Sunday-school matter—discussions of first principles of organ·

ization, management, and teaching, practical hints, reports, lists of requisites, new and suggestive "Institute" programmes, model lessons, and the best phases of our Sunday-school work.

The "Requisites" are certificates of admission and dismission, reward tickets, books of registry, catechisms, question books, hymns and music, books for teachers, maps, medals, anniversary exercises, etc.

A Normal Department has also been established by Dr. Vincent, with two courses of study—"The Church Class Course," and "The Seminary Course"—the first with three classes, "Preparatory," "Junior," and "Senior," a very thorough course, diplomas being awarded to those who finish it. Under the guidance of Dr. Vincent, that skillful superintendent, these various instrumentalities are doing great good.

Much credit is due to Dr. Wise for his "wise" and faithful labors as Secretary of the Sunday-School Union, Editor of the "Sunday-School Advocate" and of Sunday-School Books, to which he has devoted his useful life, till recently, since the General Conference of 1858, by his extensive travels, visiting the annual conferences, delivering stirring addresses, giving timely advice to the preachers, and employing his time and talents in his office at home as a "ready writer" and pleasing editor of Sunday-school literature.

At the General Conference of 1872 Dr. Vincent, with his tried skill, especially for the past four years, in the Sunday-school work, was appointed to be at the head of this important department of Church enterprise.

With all these improvements our Sunday-schools, in many sections of the Church, especially in New England, stand greatly in need of more time for their sessions. Their entire services are crowded into a brief space—from forty to sixty minutes—when every exercise must be hurried through with great rapidity, and many important matters left out.

Many of our wisest and best Sunday-school workers are hoping for the time to come when one part of our Sabbaths, now devoted to sermons, shall be used for such Sunday-school exercises as shall both please and profit not only our children, but all right-minded and intelligent adult well-wishers of the cause of God.

Should there not be also a "normal class" sustained in each of our Sunday-schools, and placed under the charge of the pastor of the Church, or his own appointed substitute, with an outline text-book—a medium between our usual question books and moral philosophy—

for the benefit of our best scholars and sharpest minds, with particular reference to their preparation for future usefulness as superintendents and teachers ? And should not also more particular attention be paid, especially in our infant and juvenile classes, to the language of the word of God, committing important and appropriate selected portions to memory? Such lessons stored in the youthful mind have produced most precious fruit for time and eternity in numerous instances.

The Church must not stop to glory in her past success when "there remains very much land to be possessed." Not only are there many children and youth whose eternal welfare may depend upon their being gathered into Sunday-schools, and there trained for Christ and heaven, but millions of adults are out of Christ, and 'out of Sunday-schools, who ought to be cared for, and, if possible, induced to attend them, and made the happy recipients of their saving benefits.

CHAPTER XII.

"Gathering Fruit unto Life Eternal."

OUR Divine Lord and Master said to his own chosen ministers, "Ye have not chosen me, but I have chosen you, and ordained you, that ye should go and bring forth fruit, and that your fruit should remain." It is with great gratitude to God that I am able to look back on my ministry and to know that, directly or indirectly, some "precious fruit" has been gathered to Christ, which remains and is recognized in the Church at the present time. I deeply regret that no more fruit has been gathered through my imperfect efforts ; but enough has been seen and acknowledged for which to be most heartily thankful to my heavenly Father. I will not here refer to more recent years, though in these I have been cheered by frequent ingatherings of "precious fruit" into "the garner of the Lord." But I wish to encourage the young laborer for Christ by referring to a few special cases in my early labors in the itinerant field, in which different persons have been brought to Christ by *special* personal efforts used—instances of conversion which have, in these many years past, had time to show their gracious results on themselves, and, through them, on many others.

In the immediate neighborhood of my early · home we had no church èdifice, and only here and there a person professing godliness, and only occasional Sabbath preaching and week-day lecture appointments by our circuit preacher. Our usual places of Church attendance were three and four miles away. In this state of religious matters our holy Christianity was at a low ebb among us.

Although my own religious life began while I was away from my early home, yet I had become most intensely interested for my friends and neighbors there. As before stated, I commenced preaching soon after I made a public profession of faith, but felt it to be a great cross to begin at home. I had held but two meetings away from home before I became conscious of a duty there which I could not evade without treachery to my Master. In accordance with my convictions, I named to a few friends that I would hold a meeting at the school-house the next evening. The news spread with great rapidity. Curiosity

brought out a crowded house. Under an inde-
scribable pressure of feeling I performed the
promised service as best I could. My gracious
Lord helped me. The word took effect. Old
professors confessed their coldness. My only
sister, some years older than myself, started for
heaven that night, and made a public statement
of her purposes. She was nearly the first one
I baptized after my ordination, and in another
town became the nucleus around which a Methodist Episcopal Church was afterward gathered.
She was " faithful unto death."

Two years after preaching my first sermon
at home our people there erected and dedicated
a church. A revival immediately commenced
which gathered in a large number. Among
those converted several dated their deep conviction back to that meeting, so memorable to
me, of two years before. One of these was my
most intimate friend and associate, a young man
with whom I had, probably, spent more hours
than with any other person not of our own
family. He stated to me afterward that he very
unexpectedly received " barbed arrows " of truth
into his heart that night which he never got rid
of till they were drawn, and the wound healed
by the Lord Jesus, at his conversion. That
young man has for some thirty-five years past

been a zealous and useful minister of the Gospel, and is now a superannuated member of the
New Hampshire Conference, preaching occasionally, as strength and opportunity will allow.
Brother J. B——, of Woodstock, Vt., is here referred to.

On old Barre Station, in Vermont, some
thirty-four years ago, I went into a school district in a remote part of the charge and held a
series of evening meetings. God graciously
blessed the effort. Some twenty souls were
gathered into the fold in a short time. The first
convert at that meeting was a young man, perhaps eighteen years old. He had a good gift and
an excellent influence. I formed a class, which
embraced the few older members of the Church
and the new recruits, among whom was that
young man's father. The young man I appointed leader. He was faithful in this duty.
Soon, feeling it to be his duty to preach, he
left the place for Newbury Seminary, preparatory to his life-work, and was licensed to preach.
This young man is now the beloved presiding
elder of Montpelier District, Vermont Conference, the Rev. J. A. S——.

Another instance of "precious fruit" gathered in my early ministry was that of a lad, I
should judge some sixteen years of age, and I

think an orphan, who lived with a Major T——
at Hanover Plain, N. H. He became a member of our Sunday-school, was greatly interested
in its exercises, and soon sought and found the
Saviour. I rejoiced to administer to him the
ordinance of baptism, and to extend to him the
hand of Church-fellowship. After a few years,
by my various removals, I lost track of him.
At length I found him in our Theological Seminary at Concord, N. H. The reader may inquire of Rev. N. M——, of the New England
Conference, for further particulars.

Other instances might be given of. gathering
ministerial fruit, of early and more recent dates,
but these must suffice. I will relate a few incidents in the ingathering of lay members into
Christ's fold.

In a certain Vermont circuit there lived a
careless neglecter of religion, the son of an in-
fidel, who taught him to despise the religion of
Christ, all the ordinances of the Church, and
her ministers. He accordingly grew up entirely
ignorant of our Church usages, and called the
ministers of the Gospel " hell-hounds." His
wife was trained a Universalist, and became
nearly as indifferent as he. Death came into
their little family, and removed from them a
beloved child. The funeral service came at

the time of our week-day quarterly meeting. Through the influence of the Divine Spirit and the afflictive providence named, " God made their hearts soft, and the Almighty troubled them." They were present at the evening prayer-meeting. I invited seekers to arise for prayers. They both quickly arose. Earnest prayer was offered for them.

The next morning they were at " love-feast." Near its close I, according to the custom of those days, gave an opportunity for any who wished to offer themselves as "probationers" for the Church. To my surprise they both readily arose. Judging that they had made a mistake, I went to them and said, " You arose to be prayed for, did you ? " They said they did. I told them the difference, when the man immediately responded, " Well, I think now I am up, I will not back out ! " I told him we sometimes took " probationers " as seekers of religion, and they could join with that under-standing if they chose. They both were so re-ceived. At the next class-meeting they were both present. When the man was spoken to he arose and said, " I don't feel as I want to ; I want to be the *first on the docket !* " The woman spoke nearly as follows : " I take great consolation. I am so glad the Lord has showed me my error. I used to think 'there wouldn't a sparrow fall,' but I am thankful to see where I have been. I take great comfort!" We said, " Thank·the Lord." " O," said she, "don't be deceived about me ! I am not converted, but I do take great consolation." We could not refrain from praising the Lord again for two more precious souls saved by grace. They proved faithful, and made good members of the Church. Years after we learned that neither had " backed out," but both were taking "great consolation," and trying to be among " the first on the docket " in their duties and privileges.

Another manifestation of saving grace was one connected with our interesting Sunday-school at Hanover some less than forty years ago. Our sisters of that Church, seeing the necessity of getting access to poor children for Sunday-school, formed a " Ladies' Sunday-School Clothing Society," with good results. Among the " clothed " was a poor girl, about twelve years old, whose father was a drunkard and mother sickly. Their poverty was extreme, and their home disagreeable by reason of rum and filth. The daughter was sought after for the Sunday-school, and respectably clothed. She became a Sunday-school scholar, made good improvement, sought and found the Saviour, to the great

joy of her heart and ours. After many years
we met her again. She was well-dressed, well-
married, and a good appearing Christian lady
living in a New England city, and, report said,
sustained a good social position there. She
introduced us to her mother, who had also become a lover of the Saviour, and greatly changed
for the better, in dress and general appearance,
from former days.

Another instance of the elevating power of
Christianity was manifested in the case of a
poor, ignorant, quarreling, hard-drinking Irish
family. There were two little children, a son,
some six or seven years old, and a daughter,
younger, in the family. I asked the parents to
let them go to our Sunday-school. They re-
pulsed me. I called again on the same errand.
They said they could not clothe them decently
to go. I offered, in behalf of the " Clothing
Society," to supply the lack of clothes. They
consented. The clothes were soon provided.
The next Sabbath morn as early as half past
nine o'clock the proud father led into our home
his two little bright-eyed, well-dressed children,
never prouder of them than then, and said to
me in his Irish brogue, " I present them to you,
sir." We took them to church, gave them seats
in the parsonage pew, and put them into good

classes in Sunday-school. Thus for weeks we took kind care of them. They behaved well, and made good progress. One day said the father to me, " How do my children behave in church? I think I must come and see." He came, and then again. At length said he, " Do you know of any one in your church who will rent me a pew? I must go to church regularly." The pew was soon found. They all became regular " church-goers." In a few months they both sought "the pearl of great price," and all came to be among our warmest friends. The next year the well-preserved clothes were presented back to the society with the saying, " We are able to clothe our own children, and these clothes will do other poor children some good." Not only did he clothe his children, but paid for his preaching also. What a change in that wretched family in the course of a few months ! The children grew up to be respected, and the parents now occupy and own a good, well-furnished house, and have a good social position in that village.

In the same place where these cases last referred to occurred there was another of a very different grade, which, by its peculiarly novel and interesting characteristics, should be here recorded. A highly intelligent, well-educated lady, who was regarded as a very decided Universalist, was employed as teacher of the village high school. I found her constantly at church on the Sabbath, and at length a member of Mrs. C.'s Bible-class, and she soon asked the privilege of coming to our house on Saturday eve, and, with the use of our books, studying her Bible-class lesson in connection with us. We sought to be courteous in our treatment of her, and cautious, perhaps over-cautious, not to molest her sentiments, as she was equally cautious never to molest ours.

A few weeks only passed away before she came in expressly to have some conversation on what to her and to us was a subject of very great interest. "I have come," said she, "to say to you that I want to join your Church. I am a Universalist, but believe I have experienced religion, and my Universalist preachers do not feed me. They do not preach Christian experience, and I am not satisfied without hearing it preached as I think I have it. You preach it as I understand it, and I think I can live religion better by joining the Church than to undertake to live out of it."

I said, "Miss H., how can you subscribe to our Church faith and usages and still be, as you say you are, a Universalist?" She readily replied, "I do not want to be tenacious about Universalism. It may be true, and may not. I think eventually all will reach heaven, but I am willing to let this be my silent belief, as I am with you in other doctrines." I replied, " Miss H., what if some day you should hear some of us preach on future and endless punishment, and when you got home your father, a most decided Universalist, should say to you, 'Well, Rosaline, have you had hell-fire and damnation preached to you to-day?' what could you say to it ? "

She respectfully answered, "I should say to him, 'Our minister preached what I have no doubt he sincerely believes, and I have no disposition to find fault with him about it.'" Being satisfied that she would be true to her Church obligations, and an ornament to the cause, I went out to consult the leader and other official members near by to learn what position they would take in her case. They all said, " Take her ; she will· know before her six months' probation is out what she is."

Returning, I reported our decision. She replied, "I thank you for your willingness to receive me, and for your thoroughness with me. I expected it, and am glad to have it so, Now I want in two weeks from next

Sabbath to be baptized at the altar and received on probation, if you are willing." This being agreed to, she then proceeded to say, "Before I go any further in this matter I shall go home and tell my father just what I have decided upon, and invite him to come and be with me when I am baptized. If it has no other effect he will respect me for my frankness and invitation."

When the time arrived she was in her place for the ordinance, but without her father. The occasion was one of special interest and profit. She from that day forth never failed in social meetings to bear testimony for Christ, never for once indicating there or elsewhere that she was a Universalist. At the end of her six months' probation she joined in full. She lived a few years a faithful and true Christian, an ornament to the Church, and died happy, greatly lamented, and beloved by all her acquaintances. Her father and other Universalist relatives, though professedly unchanged in sentiment, for Rosaline's sake ever after this spoke well of the Church of her choice.

Another interesting instance of sowing beside all waters and of gathering fruit unto life eternal is worthy of record here. It will illustrate the power of Gospel truth, providentially brought to bear upon the people of a certain parish through the silent teachings of

ONE GOOD AND USEFUL BOOK.

The place alluded to is situated on the banks of White River, Vermont, a place where Calvinistic doctrines and old Puritanic usages had almost unlimited sway thirty or forty years ago. There no other than the parish Church had place among them. The place, like ancient Jericho, was straitly shut up. No other Christian people than their own were allowed, if it was possible to prevent it, to come in to invade their pretended rights ; so said outside reports. Their parish minister was dull and prosy, his sermons long and tedious. Report said he was nearing the day of his dismissal.

This old parish was within the bounds of a certain circuit to which the writer, thirty years ago, had been a short time appointed. In one of our circuit tours, Mrs. C. being with me, we, being unacquainted with the roads, chanced to take the wrong one, and came out at the aforesaid village, where we were perfect strangers. As we came in sight of it our horse accidentally stepped upon a sharp-pointed stake, which caused it to be violently thrown up, making a

deep wound in his flesh, and causing him to
furiously run our carriage against a solid rock
at the roadside, when we were violently thrown
out, harness and wagon broken, the horse apparently bleeding to death, and, vastly worse
than all the rest, Mrs. C. was lying helpless on
the ground, and it was feared fatally wounded.

We were taken to the house of a good hospi-
table lady, where Mrs. C. was well cared for.
Here we were detained for weeks by her severe
sickness. When it was possible to remove to
our home, and our bills for board, nursing,
horse-keeping, and mending up a broken wagon
and harness were called for, we had none to pay,
except a small doctor's bill, not a fourth part
usually charged for such service rendered. The
good woman who bore the main expense accepted the present of a few good books, among
which was "Mahan on Christian Perfection."

One day Captain H. came in and found her
reading it. He asked for its title. On being
told what it was, and how she came by it, he
remarked, "Better not read it; it is Methodist heresy." She laid it aside.

Relating these facts to a live member of that
Church, he said, "Lend it to me, *I* will read
it." He took and read it; then another and
another. It set their souls on fire of love divine.

They said, "If these things are so, we must have prayer-meetings specially to pray for more religion." They were held, when others caught the flame. At length came the pastor of the Church, who also was warmed by the same influence, and preached with new power. A revival followed, converts were added to the Church, and their formerly dull minister, being as good as new, gave good satisfaction for years longer.

All this good fruit, this rich harvest, is said to have sprung from that good seed thus providentially sowed. Not Methodist heresy, but Gospel truth, published by a Presbyterian author, "brought forth fruit into life eternal."

One more reminiscence must suffice. On the Winchester Station, some twenty-five years ago, the writer called on all who would enlist for a revival of religion to meet at the parsonage the next Monday evening. Of a large Church-membership about a dozen came. The pastor presented to them a written plan for systematic personal effort to save souls, containing a pledge by which we bound ourselves to work according to the proposed plan till we should see a revival, and as much longer as we should see best. All signed it. Then we prayed for the blessing of God on the contemplated

effort. Among other things, we promised each
to select some particular one to pray and labor
for, without mentioning to each other who that
one should be, and meet once a week and report our success, and pray for each other and
for our own selected subjects for prayer. Several of us, it was afterward found, had fixed our
minds upon an intelligent, moral young gentleman, who had for some time been a Bible-class
teacher in the Sunday-school. At our second
meeting he came in and reported himself thus :
"Last Monday night, when you were praying
so earnestly for somebody, I leaned over my
garden fence, (he lived near by,) and wished I
knew if you were praying for me. I could not
help weeping. I thought if you were so earnest for me I ought to be in earnest for myself.
Thank God, I know now you were praying for
me. I have found the Saviour, and now I am
willing to take hold with you and help save
others." He nobly redeemed his pledge. Each
week, by the same personal effort, varied only
by a change of circumstances, drew to the altar
other seeking souls, who were soon " brought
into the glorious light and liberty of the Gospel," until some fifty " were added to the
Lord."

Few laymen in the Church have proved more

faithful, or have been the means of the conversion of more sinners to Christ, than has our brother in Christ, W. J. C., now a merchant in the city of Nashua, N. H.

May our young laborers in the Gospel field— ministers and lay-members—take courage from the foregoing record of successful effort for Christ to "sow by the side of the waters," that they may "gather fruit unto life eternal," "fruit that shall remain," that both the sower and the reaper may rejoice together when the "sheaves" shall be gathered into the heavenly "garner."

CHAPTER XIII.

Educational Advantages Forty Years Ago and Now.

METHODIST SEMINARIES, FEMALE COLLEGES, AND ACADEMIES.

OUR Church had, in all her borders, but five seminaries and academies forty years ago. Two of these were in New England, and three in New York. "The Wilbraham Academy," in Massachusetts, was founded in 1826, and the "Maine Wesleyan Seminary," at Kent's Hill, a few years later. Those in New York were the "East Genesee Conference Seminary," at Ovid, founded in 1824; the "Central New York Conference Seminary," at Cazenovia, established in 1825; and the "Griffith Institute," at Springfield, established in 1829. The "Newbury Seminary," in Vermont, was not founded until 1833.

The first academic institution of the Methodists in this country was established at South New Market, N. H., in the year 1817. For several years it enjoyed a good degree of prosperity. In it "Father Taylor," of "Seamen's Bethel" fame, Amos Binney, and others of note in the ministry, were once scholars. Martin Ruter, D.D., was its first principal. This school in a few years was transferred to Wilbraham, Mass. The building is now occupied as a dwelling-house and store. Now there are under the patronage of this same Church one hundred and twenty academies and seminaries in different parts of our country, manned by *eight hundred* professors, and enrolled on their catalogues are not less than twenty-two thousand students. Some two million dollars are invested in the buildings, apparatus, and books connected therewith. Thousands have gone forth from them into various useful avocations of business life, to bless mankind with their influence. Thousands more are seeking preparation in them for future and extensive usefulness.

One marked characteristic of these schools is, that each year, in most or all of them, gracious revivals of religion are enjoyed, when large numbers of our precious youth consecrate their hearts and lives to Christ, and thus seek not only mental but moral and Christian fitness for their life-work.

We will consider next the number and condition of our

COLLEGES AND UNIVERSITIES THEN AND NOW.

In New England Methodism had, forty years
ago, the Wesleyan University, at Middletown,
Conn. It was then in its infancy, having been
established but one year. Its origin is of special interest to àll lovers of education among us.
It was on this wise : The buildings had been
owned and occupied by " The Middletown Literary and Scientific Society," and were valued at
thirty thousand or forty thousand dollars. It was
offered to the New England and New York Conferences, on condition that they would add to it
forty thousand dollars more, and thereby establish a University. The offer was gladly accepted, and the money soon raised. The late
Wilbur Fisk, D.D., of blessed memory, then
principal of the Wilbraham Academy, who had
been greatly instrumental in raising the requisite funds, was elected its first president.

Just forty years ago two other colleges were
brought under the control of our Church, name-
ly, Dickinson College, at Carlisle, Pa., with J. P.
Durbin, D.D., at its head, and the Alleghany
College, at Meadville, Pa., with Martin Ruter,
D.D., for its first president.

11

Before these colleges came into being our Church labored under great disadvantages, and graduated but few of her sons. Some had entered colleges where denominational prejudices were strong against our ecclesiastical organization and doctrines. Having been nurtured by Methodist parents, they became disgusted with their sectarian surroundings, and left before graduating, or became alienated from the Church of their early preferences, and when graduating gave their influence to other denominations, or became lost to all Church attachments.

Only here and there could be found one who endured all these fiery ordeals, to which he was subjected on account of his Church preferences, and graduated true to his earlier convictions of truth and duty. Indeed, our Methodist fathers were strongly prejudiced against college-made ministers, as they called them, believing that men truly called of God, and endowed with power from on high, would, with proper care and study, whether highly educated or not, make better ministers than self-called or college-educated ones.

With these prejudices and embarrassments in their way, they were not forward to send their sons to college. Can it, therefore, be any great marvel that the denomination had no more college graduates in her ministry and membership?

What a favorable change has been wrought in these educational interests during these past forty years! We have now twenty-eight colleges and universities, conveniently located in different sections of our Church-membership, some of which are being richly endowed by our men of "princely wealth," and by the equally generous and noble contributions of the men and women of less financial ability. The last sprang into being as if by magic. "The Boston University" takes its origin from the heart and brain of the late Isaac Rich, Esq., who has left for it the ample endowment of one million dollars. It has its departments of "theology," "law," and "music" already established, and its magnificent destiny and usefulness are made sure.

These institutions are manned by more than two hundred professors, who have educated for future usefulness and graduated some thousands of young men who are now occupying, with rare exceptions, important positions in society, and exerting a wide-spreading and salutary influence in the world.

These two hundred professors, have now under their careful training more than six thousand students, who are soon to go forth to occupy equally important positions, in the Church and out of it, with those who had graduated before them. A powerful influence for good is being widely felt and acknowledged by all observers, in a higher state of mental culture and social position, in our own and other Christian Churches.

FEMALE COLLEGES.

Special attention has been directed, also, within the past forty years, by our Church to female education. In the list of educational institutions given in this chapter more than twenty were chartered as female colleges, and various others are connected with our academies and seminaries, where large numbers of ladies have been educated in all the branches of learning required, who have graduated with college honors. They are found every-where and in all departments of useful life. They are teachers in common and high schools, in seminaries and colleges. They are editors of periodicals and authors of books—missionaries in domestic and foreign fields. But more are in our best families, exerting their comparatively silent but salutary influence in their respective

home circles. Several male colleges of high repute have of late yielded to the pressing demands which have been brought to bear upon
them, and opened their doors for the admission
and education of women, and to all the benefits
and honors within their gift. Others will soon
follow the good example thus set them—a measure which an enlightened public sentiment will
yet heartily approve.

Our Church has also at her command a
funded capital, for educational purposes, of not
less than $100,000, which is committed to the
care of an able board of trustees appointed by the
General Conference, and held by them in trust
for the purpose of aiding our Church educational interests in the different parts of our
widely-extended Zion.

There has been an evident demand for years
past for a more efficient plan and better system-
atized financial equality in sustaining these institutions, and a more elevated position in our
educational matters than has heretofore existed. Such a want, it is hoped, will be met
in the provisions made at our last General
Conference for, and the appointment of, a Secretary of Education, to devote his entire time and
talents to the one business of guiding and
guarding these great Church interests.

With great unanimity our General Conference. elected to this office that learned and efficient educator, E. O. Haven, D.D., LL.D., of the North-western Wesleyan University.* It is the verdict of the Church that he is " the right man in the right place " for raising the standard of education and of imparting new life into the various departments of our educational interests.

The progress already made in endowing and sustaining our denominational schools, it is believed, has not been surpassed if equaled by any other denomination of Christians in this country.

We come now to compare the difference in the sentiment and condition of our Church with reference to

THEOLOGICAL INSTITUTIONS THEN AND NOW.

Our denomination had no theological schools within her borders forty years ago. Her prevailing sentiment was entirely against ever establishing them.

But it must not be inferred from this that our young ministers had no " theological " training. Far from this. There was a " course of study " ordered by each annual conference which all,

* See General Conference Records of 1872.

on their two years' probation in the conference, were required to study most thoroughly. It embraced the " Doctrines of the Bible," " Church Government," " Church History," and English branches.

Our text-books for careful study were the Bible, "Wesley's Sermons," " Watson's Institutes," " Fletcher's Checks," " Watson's Dictionary," " Ruter's Church History," " The Methodist Discipline," and some other books. This " course " demanded of our young ministers a thorough application of their time and talents.

He who could pass a satisfactory examination in every particular, at the termination of his two years' " *course*," before a " committee of examination," consisting of the wisest heads and closest critics in the conference, was regarded quite fortunate. To be successful he was obliged to study late and early in his temporary homes ; and having " no certain abiding place," together with his constant change of circumstances, his mode of travel, his needed preparations for the Sabbath, and numerous interruptions from study in various ways, he was compelled to resort also, at times, to barns, or shade-trees, or the thicker forests—" God's first temple "—to pursue his studies.

At the close of my first year in conference

I attended its annual session and listened to the examination of the class of that year, and found it to be exceedingly rigid. Several whom I had supposed to be well prepared for examination were pronounced by the committee to be "deficient," and were put over to another year for re-examination. This alarmed me, causing me to quicken my efforts in order to be prepared for *my* "day of trial," lest I too should share a similar fate.

When my day came the committee, to my unspeakable relief, pronounced my examination " satisfactory," and I was admitted to full membership in the conference. I have never regretted this thorough drill of those two years in that "*old-fashioned*" theological school of earlier Methodism.

About this time the subject of "*theological schools*" of the modern kind began to be agitated in the Church. It met with marked opposition from most of our ministers and members. Some prophesied if Methodism established them "her glory would depart " from her, and "*Ichabod* be written on her walls." Such schools were contemptuously denominated "minister mills," and their graduates "men-made ministers," which the mills ground out.

As the subject continued to be agitated new

advocates continued to increase in their favor, especially in the New England conferences ; but in the South and West the opposition con- tinued for a much longer time. I well remem- ber the opposition of a General Conference officer, a member of the "old Baltimore Con- ference," who visited ours. By invitation he preached to us. In the course of his sermon he uttered, apparently with great delight, the following sentiment, in nearly these words : " I have heard," said he, " of a wonderful thing un- der the sun. I have heard that men take the pure Gospel seed and carry it to a ' theological mill,' and get it ground to fine flour, and then sow it over the people, and wonder why it doesn't spring up and 'bear fruit.' " This I considered to be the echo of the opposition in the South and West to the new ideas advocated by some of our best minds in New England.

Dr. Abel Stevens had then returned from his visit to the " Wesleyan Theological School," at Hoxton, in England, and had become an enthu- siastic admirer of its order, which he regarded as "almost divine," and it had "set his heart on fire," and he determined to encourage the plan in America. Also, Dr. Stephen Olin vis- ited the same school with similar effect. So also did Dr. Wilbur Fisk, who determined to open a "theological department" in the university of which he was president. Such a department, in the midst of great opposition, was opened in the year 1838, and it continued to be open for theological students for the space of four or five years, when other means for theological training were provided.

The opposition in New England so far gave way that the trustees of Newbury Seminary, in the year 1843, opened a theological department therein, and invited Rev. Prof. William M. Willett to become its first president and teacher of Hebrew and sacred literature. This post he accepted and creditably filled. In the year 1845 John Dempster, D.D., became connected with the institute. It was soon removed to Concord, N. H., and established on a much larger scale, where it continued for some twenty years in successful operation, and then was removed to Boston, where it has become more richly endowed, and is now a theological department in the "Boston University," manned by a strong board of theological professors.

Our Church has also one in the West—the Garrett Theological Seminary, at Evanston, Ill.; another in New Jersey—the Drew Theological Seminary; and one in the South—the Clark

Theological Seminary, at Atlanta, S. C., with
Rev. J. W. Lee at its head.

At these institutions from two hundred and
fifty to three hundred young men, who claim
to be called of God to the work of the Christian ministry, are being prepared, mentally and
spiritually, for the commencement of their important life-work. Hundreds more have been
educated in them who are now doing efficient
service, at home and in the foreign fields, in the
various departments of the Lord's vineyard.

PERIODICAL LITERATURE THEN AND NOW.

American Methodism, forty years ago, had
under her patronage and control our excellent
" Quarterly Review," with a limited circulation,
mostly among the preachers. It had been
published fifteen years. We had our official
weekly organ—" The Christian Advocate and
Journal"—which had been established seven
or eight years, and one semi-official weekly—
" The Zion's Herald"—published in Boston,
Mass. This was established in 1823, and
therefore is the oldest Methodist weekly periodical in the world. I think these embrace the
entire list of our periodicals forty years ago.

What an astonishing change has taken place
in periodical literature since then, both in their

number and quality! "The Quarterly Review" has been much enlarged and greatly improved, and its circulation extensively increased. "The Christian Advocate and Journal" is much enlarged and improved, with a circulation far more extensive than then. So also has that older New England organ—"Zion's Herald"—not only changed its size and form, but has a vastly wider circulation than in its more youthful days.

Besides these, we have nine weekly official "Christian Advocates" published from the different presses of the denomination in the various localities of the country. "Zion's Herald," though never dependent on the funds of our Book Concern for support, has had from its youth a large and vigorous growth, and now, near the close of its half century, is loved and honored as equal at least to the best weekly Methodist periodicals of the Church. There are several other semi-official and official periodicals, owned by members of our Church, and patronized mainly by the denomination, which have extensive circulation in the country.

Of monthly magazines, there is the "Ladies' Repository," with its extensive circulation throughout the country. It is justly termed

" The Queen of the Monthlies." It is published at Cincinnati, O., and has reached its thirty-eighth volume. " The Golden Hours," another monthly, also published at the Western Book Room, is a *first-class* illustrated work for juveniles. The last General Conference also authorized, conditionally, the publication of a " Literary Monthly Magazine " in Boston, Mass., which is soon to appear before the reading public.

Besides the " Sunday-School Advocate," a child's paper, now ordered to be a weekly, having a circulation of more than three hundred thousand copies—the largest circulation of any like publication in the world—we have the " Sunday-School Journal," for adults, " The Sunday-School ·Bell," in the German, and the " Sunday-School Messenger," in the Swedish languages, " The Missionary Advocate," and " The Good News." All these periodicals cannot fail to produce a powerful influence for good on vast numbers of the people of our country.

What marvelous improvements in our literary advantages in the past forty years !

CHAPTER XIV.

Methodism and the Abolition of Slavery.

THE question of the immediate abolition of slavery in the United States was scarcely agitated in our Church or in the country by any class of people forty years ago. Although there were some three millions of men, women, and children held in abject bondage, recognized in law as mere goods' and chattels, and although there were some thousands of these held by southern members of the said Church, yet these facts seemed to awaken no serious alarm among our people, even in the Northern States.

In the South, Methodist slaveholders sought to justify themselves by claiming that under certain circumstances the Bible sanctioned the holding of slaves. The laws of their States allowed and shielded them in it, and the Discipline of the Church threw around them its arms of protection.

The northern members seemed to feel that it

was enough that the Church, from her origin, had recorded her decided verdict against the institution, and therefore it was the wisest policy to let it take its own course in our Church under their humane masters and the ameliorating influence of the Gospel of Christ. This was the position, as I understand it, taken by a majority of her ministers and members on this subject forty years ago.

In its confirmation I give the following extract from high authority: "The course pursued by the Methodist Episcopal Church from the beginning of her existence, in reference and in opposition to slavery, as it has all along existed in the United States, proves that she has always considered it an evil not to be tolerated, except under given circumstances, and that such circumstances exist in some portions of our Union, where such severe penal laws have been enacted against emancipation as to justify her in holding in her communion those who hold slaves, provided they are otherwise pious. That this was her doctrine is provable from the whole course of her proceeding, from the time of her organization in 1784.

"At that time were passed the severest laws against slavery which we find upon record at any time of her existence; but even these aimed at gradual, and did not insist upon immediate emancipation ; yet finding upon experiment that these severe rules could not be carried into execution without producing greater evil than that which it was designed to remove, in about six months after they were passed they were suspended and have never been revived, nor were they ever inserted in the Discipline.

"At almost every General Conference some enactment has been made for the purpose of regulating slavery, of modifying or of mitigating its character, with a view ultimately, if practicable, to do it away. This has been the doctrine, and these have been the measures of our Church in reference to this most difficult and perplexing subject ; and they prove incontestably that she does not, nor has at any time, considered slaveholding, under all circumstances, of such a deadly character as to 'exclude a man from the kingdom of grace and glory.'" *

I think this expresses the general verdict of our Church on the subject forty years ago. It was then thought to be just as high an anti-slavery position as the Church could sustain. But it is not the strong, high, and bold verdict of Methodism, as given by Wesley, when he

---

* Dr. Bangs' History of Methodism, vol. iv, for the year 1836.

declared that "Men-buyers are exactly on a level with men-stealers ;" and when to slave-holders he said, "Thy hands, thy bed, thy furniture, thy house, thy lands are at present stained with blood." Nor is it the sentiment of Dr. Adam Clarke, who said, "In heathen countries slavery was in some sort excusable, but among Christians it is an enormity and a crime, for which perdition itself has scarcely an adequate state of punishment." Nor is it in accordance with the verdict of Methodism in 1780, that is, four years before our Church was organized, when she uttered in her conference the following verdict against the peculiar institution : "Slavery is contrary to the laws of God, man, and nature, hurtful to society, contrary to the dictates of a pure conscience and pure religion, and 'doing what we would not that others should do unto us.'" And they passed their disapprobation upon all our friends who kept slaves, and advised their freedom.

When the Church was organized in 1784 she adopted the following rules : "Every member of our societies shall legally execute and record an instrument for the purpose of setting every slave in his possession free within the space of two years."

Among others was this also : "Every person

12

concerned who will not comply with these rules shall have liberty to withdraw from our Society within the twelve months following the notice being given aforesaid, otherwise the assistant shall exclude him from the Society."

Again, "Those who buy or sell slaves, or give them away unless on purpose to free them, should be expelled immediately."

Such was the verdict of Methodism in her early days ; but forty years ago not one fourth part of the article in the Discipline against slavery, which had been there thirty-two years before, remained. The General Conferences from time to time had so modified the terms of membership, and widened the door to such an extent, that slaveholders could easily enter and peacefully stay in her communion. Hence forty years ago slavery had acquired a strong position in the Church as well as in the nation.

This was our sad condition as a Church when the abolition agitation began among us. It first took strong hold upon our Methodism in the New Hampshire and New England Conferences. The large majority of our ministers and lay members became abolitionists in some two years after the agitation began.

In the year 1835, when our delegates to the General Conference were chosen in these Con-

ferences, it was found that all in the New
Hampshire, and all but two in the New England Conference, were abolitionists. These
constituted "the immortal fourteen," who stood
up manfully for the cause in the midst of a
powerful opposition in the General Conference
of 1836.

At the General Conference of that year two
delegates, both members of the New Hampshire
Conference, Revs. George Storrs and Samuel
Norris, had taken the liberty to go into an antislavery meeting in the city of Cincinnati, where
its session was held, and had expressed freely
their abolition sentiments therein, for which act
they were severely censured by the conference.
Resolutions of censure were offered, and, after a
most exciting discussion, were almost unanimously adopted. "The immortal fourteen," as
they were often afterward called, and these only,
stood up for the right, and answered to their
names when called by their emphatic nays
against the unjust action. This resolution remained on its journal till 1868, when, in the
General Conference of that year, Rev. L. D.
Barrows, D.D., as chairman of the Committee
on the State of the Church, presented a resolution to expunge it from the records, which was
adopted.

So fearfully ran the excitement in the General Conference of 1836, that some of the members of that body feared, or at least claimed to fear, that the *gross* offense of the offending two would be the cause of creating a mob, and thus bring their great ecclesiastical council into disrepute. The censured members, however, survived the shock, and antislaveryism continued to spread more and more both in and out of the Church, though its advocates were proscribed, and all manner of efforts were put forth to cause them to " cease agitating the subject."

The position of affairs in the Church on this subject at that time is correctly set forth in the following extract from a letter written by one of " the *immortal fourteen* " above referred to : " Respecting the origin of abolitionism in the Church," says he, " I distinctly recollect that O. Scott, Geo. Storrs, J. Horton, and L. Sunderland were in the field as lecturers, and led the van among the Methodists, accompanied by J. A. Merrill, P. Crandall, J. F. Adams, Elihu Scott, A. D. Merrill, and other less prominent but effective workers in the cause. These were contemporaries with Wm. L. Garrison, J. Leavitt, J. G. Birney, Garret Smith, and others of note, for a year or two previous to the General Conference of 1836. Till then the

abolitionists in the Church had been confined
to New England. The two conferences—New
Hampshire and New England—had acquired a
majority, and chose abolition delegates to that
conference.

Here, for the first time, abolitionism became
a disturbing element in the counsels of the
highest judicatory of the Methodist Episcopal
Church. Though their number was small, their
heroism having been tested in their own annual
conferences, their influence was felt in debate
on the floor of the General Conference. In
attempting to crush them by a sweeping resolution denouncing " modern abolitionism," fourteen voters stood up to record their names in
opposition.

It seems difficult, even at this short space of
time since the abolition of slavery in the nation,
to realize the kind and degree of prejudice that
then prevailed against the abolitionists. They
were supposed to be composed of about equal
parts of *fanaticism* and *insanity*, which was
deemed a sufficient reason for commanding them,
by the authorities of the Church, to " wholly refrain" from agitating the subject of slavery,
for restricting them in the prestige of their
appointments in the conference, and in prevent-
ing others from becoming members at all, which

was repeatedly done without any disguise because of their abolitionism. But they were not
charged with any moral wrong, and, therefore,
not subjects of any judicial punishment ; but.
were looked upon, rather, with a kind of pitiful
detestation, akin to that which the community
feel toward the Mormons or the soul-blighting
annihilationists. Hence, while the General
Conference could condemn abolitionism, and
vote a strong disapproval of her members attending abolition prayer-meetings, their chief
speakers were very earnest to disclaim any im-
putation against the motives of their troublesome opponents ; and while wishing them in
heaven,* to get them out of their way, they
explicitly acknowledged that they believed that
they were well prepared for that place. †

After that General Conference the agitation
went on increasing more and more, East, West,
North, and South, both in the Church and out
of it, and the more the question was agitated
the more the sentiments of " modern abolitionists " gained volume, force, and respectful attention among high-minded and humane people. .

* See pamphlet entitled "Debates on Modern Abolitionism"
in General Conference of 1836.

† Letter by Rev. S. Norris to the author, dated August 5,
1872.

In 1844 the General Conference held its session in New York, when the delegates struck a severe blow against slaveholding in our Church in several ways ; one of which was in the confirmation by that body of the verdict of the Baltimore Conference by which they expelled Rev. F. A. Harding from their communion on account of his having been found to be a slaveholder.

Another blow struck against " the peculiar institution," and slaveholding by the Church, was in the verdict which that body pronounced against Bishop Andrew, who had (by his wife) become virtually a slaveholder. A resolution was offered requesting him to cease his official relation as a bishop in the Church while he held slaves. The resolution was discussed by pro-slavery and antislavery members for days together with great ability and warmth, the Border and Middle States men taking strong antislavery ground, rendering it a matter of policy for the so-called " modern abolitionists " to be comparatively quiet, and for those who had been regarded not so radical to carry on the aggressive warfare they had so manfully commenced.

The resolution of censure at length passed by a large majority, which produced a fearful excitement and alienation among the southern members and their pro-slavery friends. They immediately struck for Church division, a virtual secession from the parent Church. A conditional plan for the division was immediately offered to that body, and after much discussion agreed upon, by which nearly half a million ministers and lay members went off and formed what was and now is called " The Methodist Episcopal Church, South," though the conditions of the plan were never complied with.

This measure was a severe blow, struck by the South to weaken the bonds of our national union of States, leaving the southern Church free from the restraints of antislavery to become more and more radical in their pro-slavery position, and also the Methodists in the North, with but few slaves and less slaveholders, to exert a stronger antislavery influence, and greater freedom to pursue their onward march to final victory.

Soon the Methodist Church became so thoroughly antislavery, even abolition, in sentiment that the verdict of her annual and General Conferences was decidedly in condemnation of the " peculiar institution," though some slaveholders still were suffered to retain their relation to the Church.

In 1861 the South struck another blow—a fatal one—against their own cherished institution by raising its rebellious arms against the Northern States. This aroused the spirit of loyalty and freedom in the North, and with the colored people of the South, when, with all other good citizens, loyal Methodism performed an honorable and heroic part in providing our country with soldiers for our defense, nurses for our hospitals, sanitary provisions for our sick and wounded, and in offering her prayers to heaven for the victory of our arms.

Abraham Lincoln, then our wise and observant chief magistrate, and now lamented ex-President, bore this honorable and deserved testimony of our Church at the time : " Nobly sustained as the government has been by all the Churches, I would utter nothing which might in the least appear invidious against any. Yet without this, it may fairly be said that the Methodist Episcopal Church, not less devoted than the best, is, by its greater numbers, the most important of all.

" It is no fault in others that the Methodist Church sent more soldiers to the field, more nurses to the hospitals, and more prayers to heaven than any. God bless the Methodist Church ! bless all the Churches ! and blessed be

God • who in this great trial giveth us the Churches !" *

In 1863 came the last expiring groans of the iniquitous system of American slavery by the lamented President's proclamation of freedom to all the slaves of our country, by which the last fetter was broken off from every bondman. It was then "Jehovah had triumphed and the negro was free."

This was needful to save the country. It gave the colored race a powerful motive to en- list in the bloody strife for our nation's safety, and also a new impetus to all loyal hearts. By it our Church was saved from further debate on the abolition question, for her slave-bound mem- bers were raised to a civil and ecclesiastical level with their former masters, however pleas- ant or unpleasant the recognition of the fact to the latter.

Now after this forty years' struggle with this "abomination of desolation ;" after the sad havoc of Churches, and doubtless loss of souls by the southern Church secession in 1844 ; after all the strife and contention arising therefrom in regard to Church property and Church terri-

* Extract of a letter by President Lincoln to the General Confereuce in 1864. See " Stevens' Centenary of Methodism," pp. 210, 211.

tory ; after the terribly bloody war of rebellion, we can but rejoice to find the colored man in our State and national Legislatures, and in other high governmental positions. We find him, also, in our annual conferences, even with whole conferences under his control mainly, and in the General Conference, taking important parts in debates, and taking other responsible positions in its business matters.

What a marvelous change in these forty years past !

CHAPTER XV.

Lay Delegation Forty Years Ago and Now.

THERE was a strong prejudice against lay representation in the General and Annual Conferences forty years ago. The exciting discussions on the subject which had preceded, attended, and followed the different secessions from our Church had awakened great opposition to it in the minds of those who were reckoned among her most loyal and worthy members. There were then "the Reformed Methodist" and "the Protestant Methodist" Churches, which made lay representation a prominent feature in their Church polity. A bitter spirit had been infused into these new denominations by the leading seceders, which was retained for many years. Under these circumstances it was extremely difficult for our people to see any special advantages which could result from a change in our Church polity, especially as she was constantly making more rapid progress than were the seceding Churches.

The misnamed Boston " Olive Branch," their New England organ, extended no "olive branch" of "peace and good will" to us, but waged a constant warfare against our form of Church government and its advocates.

Surrounded with such opposing influences, it may not appear strange that any of our ministers or lay members would have been regarded as disloyal to the Church of their choice who could be found advocating the introduction of this new element into our Church government.

A few years later we witnessed the strife, heard the debates, and read the newspaper controversies on the subject connected with the so-called " True Wesleyan Secession," when a large number of our preachers and members left us and organized the Wesleyan Methodist Church with the lay element in its polity. By this secession some of our Churches were entirely broken up, and others greatly weakened. Can' there be any wonder, then, that our true and loyal members, seeing these results, looked upon lay delegation with special disfavor?

These stormy discussions and adverse scenes in a few years passed away, leaving a clearer sky and purer atmosphere. Our people then began to take the subject into more candid and careful consideration, when it became apparent that among our ministers and lay members were many advocates for the new measure, provided it could be accomplished without Church ruptures and in brotherly love. This sentiment gradually increased among our people. New advocates, truly loyal to the Church, constantly appeared publicly vindicating the idea, until " the leaven " of lay representation was found to have diffused itself through the whole Church.

Petitions, numerously signed, were sent up to each succeeding General Conference, until it was seen to be the general voice of our Church· that the change should be made in her polity. These petitions were carefully considered and judiciously acted upon by the several General Conferences.

The one held in Chicago in 1868 adopted the following " Plan" for the action of the lay members and the Annual Conferences :

PLAN OF LAY DELEGATION ADOPTED BY THE
GENERAL CONFERENCE.

"*Whereas*, the General Conference of 1860 expressed its willingness to admit lay delegates to the General Conference whenever the people should desire it ; and, whereas, the General Conference of 1864 concurred in that action ; therefore,

"*Resolved*, That we also concur in the same, and recommend the following plan to the godly consideration of our ministers and people.

"Change the Discipline, page 45, part ii, chapter 1, section 1, so that it shall read as follows:

"*Q.* Who shall compose the General Conference, and what are the regulations and powers belonging to it?

"*Ans.* 1. The General Conference shall be composed of ministerial and lay delegates. The ministerial delegates shall consist of one member for every thirty members of each annual conference, to be appointed either by seniority or choice, at the discretion of such annual conference, yet so that such representatives shall have traveled at least four full calendar years from the time that they were received on trial by an annual conference, and are in full connection at the time of holding the conference.

"The lay delegates shall consist of two laymen for each annual conference, except such conferences as have but one ministerial delegate, which conferences shall be entitled to one lay delegate.

"The lay delegates shall be chosen by an electoral conference of laymen, which shall assemble for the purpose on the third day of the

session of the annual conference, at the place
of its meeting, at its session immediately preceding the General Conference. The electoral
conference shall bé composed of one layman
from each circuit or station within the bounds
of the annual conference, and, on assembling,
the electoral conference shall organize by electing a chairman and secretary of their own
number ; such laymen to be chosen by the last
quarterly conference preceding the time of its
assembling ; *provided*, that no layman shall be
chosen a delegate either to the electoral conference or to the General Conference who shall
be under twenty-five years of age, or who shall
not have been a member of the Church in full
connection for the five consecutive years preceding the elections.

"After Answer 3, as follows, paragraph 46.

"*Ans.* 3. At all times when the General
Conference is met it shall take two thirds of the
whole number of ministers and lay delegates to
form a quorum for transacting business. The
ministerial and lay delegates shall sit and de-
liberate together as one body, but they shall
vote separately, whenever such separate vote
shall be demanded by one third of either order,
and in such cases the concurrent vote of both
bodies shall be necessary to complete an action.

"*Resolved,* That during the month of June, 1869, on any day except the Sabbath, the time to be determined by the pastor and two laymen appointed by the quarterly conference, as hereafter provided, there shall be held a general election in the several places of worship of the Methodist Episcopal Church, at which all members in full connection, and not less than twenty-one years of age, shall be invited to vote by ballot '*for Lay Delegation,*' or '*against Lay Delegation.*'

"This election shall be held under the direction of the preacher in charge, and two laymen appointed for the purpose by the quarterly conference, who shall see that due notice is given thereof for at least twenty days before the election, and who shall superintend all the details of the election.

"They shall report the result within ten days after the election to the presiding elder of the district, who shall report the same to the bishop presiding at the ensuing annual conference, to be entered upon the conference journal.

"It shall be the duty of the bishops presiding at the several annual conferences, at their first sessions after the above elections, to lay before those bodies the following proposed amendments to the second restrictive rule, namely, At the end of line third, after the word 'one' insert the word 'ministerial,' (page 47 of the Discipline,) and after the word 'forty-five,' line 7, same page, add the words, 'nor more than two lay delegates for any annual conference,' and to report the result to the next General conference as amended, so that as amended it shall read :

" 'They shall not allow of more than one ministerial representative for every fourteen members of the annual conference, nor allow of a less number than one for every forty-five, nor more than two lay delegates for any annual conference.'

"*Resolved,* That should a majority of the votes cast by the people be in favor of Lay Delegation, and should three fourths of all the members of the annual conferences present and voting thereon vote in favor of the above proposed change in the constitution of the Church, then the General Conference meeting in 1872, by the requisite two thirds vote, can complete the change, and lay delegates previously elected may then be admitted."

This "Plan" was accordingly submitted to the annual conferences, and lay membership, according to its provisions, and received their required sanction.

The quarterly conferences elected their delegates to their respective "lay electoral conferences," which met according to the prescribed "Plan," and each elected two laymen to represent it in the next General Conference.

This ecclesiastical council of our Church most cheerfully opened its doors for their reception, and gave them its hearty welcome as "brethren beloved," and on equal terms with the ministerial delegates. Among these laymen were seven ex-governors, two United States senators, nine judges and ex-judges, two college professors, eleven bankers, and many lawyers, merchants, physicians, manufacturers, and farmers, all of whom rendered efficient services on committees and in the deliberations and decisions of this, our highest Church tribunal.

Many who looked upon this measure "with fear and trembling" have had their fears removed, and now all the Church, or nearly all, "thank God and take courage," under the full conviction that "*Lay Delegation*" is for His glory and the general good of his cause. A happy termination is this of many years of loyal Christian effort!

CHAPTER XVI.

Numerical Strength of Methodism Forty
Years Ago and Now—General Statistics
Then and Now.

THE numerical strength of our Church
forty years ago was found to consist of
some two thousand and ten preachers and
five hundred and thirteen thousand one hundred
and fourteen members. This number (of course)
included all, both in the North and in the
South, the Church then not having been divided. This was the rapid growth of sixty-six
years, that is, from 1766 (the year the first class
was formed, which consisted of five members)
to the year 1832.

When we take into consideration the facts
that these five were Irish emigrants who lived
in comparative poverty and obscurity in New
York City; the constant hinderances thrown in
their way by the depleting effects of the Revo-
lutionary war and the war of 1812; the poverty
of the people; the strong hold other and older
Churches had secured; and the powerful preju-

dices which had been created in the public mind against Methodism, we must regard this increase as very remarkable. It was "not by" human "might, nor by power, but by the Spirit of the Lord." "Paul planted, Apollos watered, but *God* gave the increase." Since then our increase has been still more marvelous. Now, after forty years, the Church numbers some *ten thousand* traveling preachers and more than this number of local preachers, and near a *million and a half* of lay members.

This increase has been secured notwithstanding the "Southern secession" of near half a million of members in 1844, and the "True Wesleyan secession" of a few years before. In the past forty years her increase has been (after all these secessions) about one million members. This is a more steady and rapid increase than that of any other denomination of evangelical Christians in America. Our present increase is at the rate of one thousand seven hundred per week. But this even does not show to us all the numerical force of Methodism in these United States.

If we reckon the members of all the different branches of Church organizations which bear the name of Methodist in this country, we find a numerical strength of more than three millions.

These have all sprung from one head—John Wesley—and are all one in doctrine, though differing in some features of Church polity, but are yearly becoming more closely united in their fraternal relations to each other. The time is looked for, by many careful observers of " the signs of the times," when the entire forces of Methodism in our country shall be in harmonious fellowship, and perhaps embraced in one denominational fold.

There is no doubt in the minds of those who have an opportunity to judge impartially that ten millions, or one fourth, of the people of these United States have their preference for, and denominational attachment to, Methodism. This is the result of a little more than a century of sacrifice and toil in this country.

In the world at large Methodism numbers more than four millions of lay members, and more than fifteen millions of hearers, though her entire history covers a period of only some one hundred and thirty-three years. " What hath God wrought" by this instrumentality! Even in 1860 * Dr. Abel Stevens' estimate of Methodism numerically was, that the membership could not be less than three millions when all the missionary stations were included, and

* See " Christian Advocate and Journal," 1860.

that her hearers did not fall far below twelve millions.

Let us now consider our

METHODISTIC NUMERICAL GROWTH IN THE NORTH-WEST.

Although the great valley of the Mississippi was getting to be a stronghold of Methodism forty years ago, yet in the more newly settled portions of the great North-west our people had then but a feeble beginning. The first classes formed in Illinois were in Plainfield and in Galena, in the year 1829. The first in Chicago was in 1831. This was the *third* class formed in Northern Illinois. The first church edifice in the State was at Galena, just forty years ago. The first sermon ever preached in Chicago was by a Methodist preacher by the name of Isaac Scarritt, in the year 1829.

From these small beginnings Methodism took a wide spread throughout the North-west. Rev. John Sinclair, who was appointed to the Chicago District in 1833, and had spent most of his life in the State, and had traveled extensively, says, " I never yet succeeded in reaching a new settlement before some other Methodist minister got in before me."

So rapid has been the progress of Methodism

in Illinois for the past forty years, that in 1870 *
there were one thousand one hundred and forty-five church edifices, one hundred and ten
thousand four hundred and ninety-nine Church
members, and one thousand six hundred and
forty-one Sunday-schools, with an enrollment of
one hundred and eighteen thousand five hundred and eighty-two officers, teachers, and
scholars.

In Michigan the same year there were four
hundred and twenty-three traveling and four
hundred and seventy-five local preachers, and a
Church membership of one hundred and sixty-
two thousand four hundred. Other parts of
the North-west are being filled up with Methodists as rapidly.

OUR GERMAN WORK—THE GROWTH OF FORTY
YEARS.

William Nast, an educated, talented, and enterprising young German emigrant, left his
' fatherland " full of the infidelity of his native
country, and sought a home, as did many others,
in the United States. He was soon awakened
most powerfully to feel the need of that Saviour
whom he had persistently rejected. He ear-

* See Methodist Almanac for 1870.

nestly sought and soon found him whom his soul sought after, " Jesus of Nazareth," by whom he was divinely regenerated and saved. Soon he began to proclaim to his German associates what Christ had done for him, and to invite them to come and " taste and see that the Lord is good." Thus, almost before being aware of it, he began to preach the glorious Gospel of Christ to his fellow-countrymen in their own language.

He was the first American convert from " the fatherland " among the Methodists ; at least the first who made an impression on the German mind. But the result, in this case, was great and glorious. The work soon spread among them with great rapidity and power. German Methodist preachers have been raised up in large numbers, who preach the word of life to our German population, while others have gone back to their " fatherland " to proclaim the good news of Gospel grace there. A foreign mission was commenced there in 1849 which is one of our most fruitful fields in any foreign land.

We have now, in the United States and in Germany, not less than forty thousand German Church members. The following statement of their number and condition is from a German source :

202 *Methodism Forty Years Ago and Now.*

" We have in America 380 traveling preachers ; 320 local preachers ; 27,431 members ; 4,265
probationers ; 476 churches, worth $1,551,700 ;
210 parsonages, worth $272,050 ; 564 Sunday-
schools ; 5,745 Sunday-school teachers ; 28,473
Sunday-school scholars, and 63,768 volumes in
libraries.

" In Germany and Switzerland, 52 traveling
preachers ; 28 local preachers ; 6,002 members ;
1,369 probationers ; 28 churches, worth $296,-
993 ; 25 parsonages, worth $12,000 ; 207 Sun-
day-schools ; 866 teachers ; 9,216 Sunday-school
scholars, and 2,341 volumes in libraries. Total,
432 traveling preachers ; 349 local preachers ;
39,157 members and probationers ; 512 churches,
worth $1,848,693 ; 235 parsonages, worth $284,-
050 ; 771 Sunday-schools ; 37,689 Sunday-school
scholars, and 66,109 volumes in libraries.

" We have two colleges, one in Berea, Ohio,
and one in Warrenton, Mo. ; one Normal School
in Galena, Ill. ; one Mission Institute in Frank-
fort-on-the-Main, in Germany ; and one Mission
House at New York.

" We also have two orphan asylums, one in
Berea, Ohio, with 65 orphans, and one in Warrenton, Mo., with 34 orphans. The running expenses of these orphan asylums come to nearly
$14,000 per year, which amount is contributed

by German Methodists. The value of the property of these institutions is over $250,000, be-
sides an endowment fund of $55,000 of the Ger-
man Wallace College at Berea, Ohio.

" I compared the contributions of American
and German members of the Methodist Episcopal Church in 1870, and found the following
results :

	American, per member.	German, per member.
Missions	45½ cents.	60 cents.
· Church Extension	5 "	32 "
Tract Society	1½ "	3 "
Bible Society	6 "	5¼ "
Sunday-School Union ..	1½ "	3½ "
Fifth Collection	9¼ "	11½ "
Total	68¾	115¼

" During the last four years the contributions
in America only to the various causes amounted to $66,829 73 for Missions, $43,609 81 for
Church Extension, $3,570 30 for Tract Society,
$6,756 23 for Bible Society, $3,456 15 for Sunday-School Union, $13,620 66 for Fifth Collec-
tion. During the same time over 14,000 adults
and children were baptized, and nearly 1,600
members were transferred by death from the ·
Church militant to the Church triumphant in
heaven.

" The circulation of the ' Christian Apologist '
is 16,000, of the ' Sunday-School Bell,' (Ger-

man Sunday-school paper,) 26,000 ; the 'Berean Lesson,' in German, 12,000. There is an almost unanimous desire throughout the German Church for a religious monthly family magazine in the German language for the use of families, Sunday-school teachers, and the youth. May we soon have it !

" The Lord bless the Methodist Church in all its branches, especially the work among the Germans in this country and the fatherland ! May the 781 German preachers and the 39,157 members continue to fight the battle of the Lord ! May they grow in faith and grace, and be inspired by the Holy Ghost, so that they all and every one shall be instruments of spreading the Gospel, and leading thousands more of their countrymen to Jesus the Saviour of sinners !" *

THE GENERAL CONFERENCES FORTY YEARS AGO
AND NOW.

The General Conference of 1832 was composed of one delegate for every five members from each of the nineteen annual conferences. It gave them one hundred and ninety-nine delegates. This ratio of representation was created twenty-four years before, when the dele-

* German correspondent in General Conference "Daily Advocate."

gated General Conference plan was first adopted. This ratio could not be changed without the concurrent voice of all the conferences and a two-third vote of the General Conference. Various attempts to change it had been made, but heretofore had failed. At this General Conference it was changed to one delegate for every fourteen members. This reduced the next General Conference delegations to one hundred and forty-eight members, making a reduction of fifty-one, notwithstanding there were three more conferences represented, and the membership had increased in the four years more than one hundred thousand.

In 1872 the General Conference had two hundred and ninety-two clerical members, and one hundred and twenty-nine lay delegates; in all, four hundred and twenty-one. They came from seventy-two conferences, embracing a membership of but little less than one million and a half.

The ratio of representation was one for every thirty members of conference, and two lay delegates for every lay electoral conference. This General Conference changed again the ratio to one for every forty-five of the annual conference members, and left the lay representation the same as before. They also created four additional conferences, making now in all seventy-six.

Though the ratio has been reduced sevenfold since the year 1832, yet the clerical delegates have increased nearly one third. These, with the lay representation, gave the General Conference of 1872 the right to two hundred and thirty-seven more than forty years before. During this time the annual conferences have increased, including the General Conferences of 1832 and 1872, from nineteen to seventy-six, an increase of fourfold.   .

Still new fields are constantly opening in the new settlements of the great West, and in the now free South, for our Church enlargement. New conferences in four years more, to meet the demands of the work, will need to be organized, and many older conferences, by the reason of their rapid increase, will need to be divided. What wonders of grace have been and are yet to be wrought through Methodism in the name and through the merits of our Lord Jesus Christ!

CHAPTER XVII.

Bishops of the Methodist Episcopal Church.

IN the year 1832, when the General Conference assembled, there were only four bishops in all, one of whom—William M'Kendree—on account of his great age and increasing infirmities, was excused from active service. He was our first American-born bishop—elected in 1808, served the Church in the high office twenty-seven years, and died in Tennessee, March 5, 1835, at the age of seventy-eight years. "He was a good man, full of faith and the Holy Ghost," and an energetic and judicious general superintendent in the Church. His dying testimony was, "All is well."

The others were Robert R. Roberts, elected in 1816, and died March 28, 1843. He was an eloquent preacher and efficient officer in the Church. Joshua Soule, elected in 1824. After serving the Church of his choice in this capacity twenty-two years he seceded and went

to the "Church South," where he died in
March, 1867, having served the Church there
for twenty-two years more. Elijah Hedding,
elected in May, 1824, and served the Church
in his high office for thirty years. He died
in great peace, at Poughkeepsie, N. Y., April
9, 1852, aged seventy-two. He was an able
preacher, a wise counselor, and unsurpassed in
his knowledge of Methodistic law and usage.

At this General Conference, in 1832, the
Episcopal Board was strengthened by the election and consecration of two additional bishops. These were John Emory and James O.
Andrew.

Bishop Emory was a thoroughly educated
man, possessed of a discriminating mind and
comprehensive judgment, giving great promise
for the future. But these high hopes were
soon cut off. He started from his home in
Baltimore, December 16, 1835, on official duties, when, his horse taking fright,. he was
thrown from his carriage with great violence,
fatally injured, and soon died, aged forty-eight
years.

James O. Andrew served as bishop in the
Methodist Episcopal Church till 1844, when he
received the censure of the General Conference
for becoming identified with slaveholding by

reason of his wife's having property in them,
when he and most of the southern ministers
and members withdrew, and organized what
was called the " Methodist Episcopal Church,
South."

It may be well here to give a brief statement
of the bishops who had preceded those of forty
years ago. They were Thomas Coke, LL.D.,
Francis Asbury, Richard Whatcoat, and Enoch
George. Bishop Coke of the British Conference, and of English birth, was ordained by
Mr. Wesley in 1784, and sent over to our
country as "General Superintendent" of American Methodism. He labored faithfully in his
office for a few years, but devoted the latter
part of his valuable life to the superintendency of Wesleyan Missions. After crossing
the Atlantic Ocean eighteen times in connection with his great work, he died at sea,
May 4, 1814, greatly loved and lamented by
all lovers of the cause to which he had devoted
his life.

Bishop Asbury, selected for the office by Mr.
Wesley as joint superintendent with Dr. Coke,
declined to accept the honorable position unless
the American brethren would vote to ratify the
appointment. At the Christmas Conference of
that year—1784—his decision was duly pre-
14

sented, when he was elected and consecrated to the sacred office, Bishop Coke officiating. Bishop Asbury had previously labored heroically in this his adopted country for three years, and continued to toil for and with his American brethren until his death, which occurred in Virginia, March 31, 1816. His age was seventy-one years.

Richard Whatcoat, another Wesleyan preacher, who was sent over to America by Mr. Wesley as a missionary a few years before, was elected bishop in the year 1800, and died, six years after, in Delaware, aged seventy-one years.

Enoch George, our second American-born bishop, was elected and consecrated in 1816, and died August 28, 1828. This was the first death among American-born bishops.

"Bishops Asbury, Whatcoat, and McKendree were never married. They lived and died without a home. They traversed the nation, preaching daily as they went in churches, in court-houses, in kitchens, in barns, and in forests. Their allowance for support was no larger than that of the humblest itinerant. Except McKendree, they had no property when they died, save what they carried about their persons on their routes."

Bishop George was no less zealous and self-sacrificing than his seniors in office.* He was a man of great simplicity of manners, a very pathetic and powerful preacher, greatly beloved in life and lamented in death.†

Within the space of the last forty years what havoc has death made of our Methodist-American bishops! Mention has already been made of five who had then passed away to their reward on high.

Of the eleven elected between 1832 and 1872, six have departed this life to join in the employments of heaven with those who had gone before. I am constrained to give names and dates.

Beverly Waugh, elected to the holy office in 1836, died in Maryland, February 9, 1865, aged sixty-nine years.

Leonidas L. Hamline, elected in 1844, resigned his office in 1852 on account of feeble health. He died in Iowa, March 22, 1865.

Osmon C. Baker, elected in 1852, died in. Concord, N. H., December 20, 1871, aged fifty-nine years.

Davis W. Clark, made bishop in 1864, died in Cincinnati, O., in 1871.

* See Stevens' " Memorials of Methodism."
† See Dr. Bangs' " History of the M. E. Church."

Edward Thomson, chosen in 1864, departed this life in Wheeling, W. Va., March 20, 1870.

Calvin Kingsley, elected in 1864, "ceased at once to work and live," in Beyroot, Syria, April 6, 1870.

These were all good, true, and able ministers of the Gospel, and wise and efficient general superintendents of the Church, whose deaths made vacancies in the bench of bishops which were difficult to fill.

The General Conference of 1872 began its important session with only one more bishop than the number the General Conference had at its commencement forty years before, and now, as then, one of these, by reason of age and infirmities, was excused from service. The four others, called effective bishops, were nearly worn out with the extra labors demanded by reason of the death of their late co-laborers. The care of all the seventy-two conferences, besides the mission fields, had proved too much for the strongest of them to endure.

This General Conference very properly voted to strengthen the episcopal board by the choice of eight additional bishops. The choice, with unusual unanimity, centered upon the following brethren, namely :

Thomas Bowman, D.D., President of the Indiana Asbury University.

William L. Harris, D.D., LL.D., Assistant Secretary of the Missionary Society of the Methodist Episcopal Church.

Randolph S. Foster, D.D., LL.D., President of the Drew Theological Seminary, Madison, N. J.

Isaac W. Wiley, D.D., editor of the " Ladies' Repository," Cincinnati, O.

Stephen M. Merrill, D.D., editor of " Western Christian Advocate," Cincinnati, O.

Edward G. Andrews, D.D., pastor Seventh Avenue Church, Brooklyn, New York East Conference.

Gilbert Haven, D.D., editor of " Zion's Herald," Boston, Mass.

Jesse T. Peck, D.D., recent pastor of Methodist Episcopal Church, Syracuse, N. Y., and author of the volume entitled " The True Woman."

They were duly consecrated " by the imposition of the hands " of the senior bishops, and are now doing efficient service in their new office for Christ and his Church. May they be eminently useful in the " high vocation " to which they are called !

In the foregoing list of bishops, including the

living and the dead, we need to add those of African descent, whose jurisdiction was limited to Africa, namely, Thomas Burns and John Wright Roberts,. of the Liberia Conference. Bishop Burns was elected to the important office in 1856, consecrated by our American bishops in 1858, and labored faithfully in his specified mission field until he died, April 18, 1863, while in Baltimore, Md.

Bishop Roberts, of that conference, was elected in 1864, and consecrated by American bishops in 1866. His residence is Monrovia, Africa. A strong desire had been expressed on the part of many to take off the restriction which limited his jurisdiction to Africa, and make him full bishop, equal in his extent of territory and authority with the other bishops; but the fact of his long residence in Africa, and that he was unknown by face to the members of the General Conference, had an adverse influence on the members of that body, and the effort failed of success.

Petitions also, numerously signed by colored conferences and colored laymen from the South, were presented to the General Conference to secure the election of a bishop of African descent to be especially devoted to the interests of the colored people of the South. This measure was also advocated by some of our ablest men in the connection, both in some of our periodicals and in the General Conference, asking not only to have him employed in the superintendence of our colored conferences in the South, but to take an equal part with the episcopal board in every part of our widely-extended Zion.

A special committee of the General Conference was created to consider this important subject. This committee was very judiciously made up of wise and able men, strong friends of the colored people, two of whom were of African blood. Their secretary was then and now is a very earnest and efficient missionary among the Freedmen of the South. The following important report was made by them on the subject, which was ably discussed and with great unanimity adopted by the General Conference.

BISHOPS OF AFRICAN DESCENT.

" The special committee to which was referred the memorial of the New Orleans Preachers' Meeting of May 23, asking for the election of an additional bishop who should be of African descent, respectfully report that, at a meeting of the committee held May 30, the statements of the memorialists and their requests were carefully considered. The very reasonable demand that at least ' some action may be taken which shall assure our people that the Methodist Episcopal Church invites to her altars peoples of every nation, and extends to them equal rights in her worship and government,' was responded to with great unanimity by the following declaration of facts, which we are persuaded will be entirely satisfactory to the memorialists :

" 1. A memorial from the preachers of the Louisiana Conference, with others, in behalf of a bishop of African descent, were promptly referred to the Committee on Episcopacy, carefully considered, and reported on as follows : ' The Committee on Episcopacy respectfully report to the General Conference, concerning the election of colored bishops, that they are deeply impressed with the Christian spirit manifested by those memorializing the General Conference on this subject. The rapid progress our brethren of color are making in all that elevates mankind is most commendable, and we have no doubt there is a future of great promise before them. Your committee would further report that, in their judgment, there is nothing in race, color, or former condition that is a bar to an election to the episcopacy, the true course being for us to elect only such persons as are by their pre-eminent piety, endowments, culture, general fitness, and acceptability, best qualified to fill the office.'

" 2. The claims of our numerous and noble-hearted membership of African descent to a perfect equality of relations with all others in our communion are fully recognized by the Discipline, and amply demonstrated in the ad- · ministration of the Methodist Episcopal Church. There is no word ' white,' to discriminate against race or color, known in our legislation ; and being of African descent does not prevent membership with white men in annual conferences, nor ordination at the same altar, nor appointment to the presiding eldership, nor election to the General Conference, nor eligibility to the highest offices in the Church.

" 3. Election to the office of bishop, from among candidates who are mutually equal, cannot be determined on the ground of color or any other special consideration. It can only be by fair and honorable competition between the friends of the respective candidates. And yet the presentation of a well-qualified man of African descent would doubtless secure very general support in view of the great interests of the Church, which would thereby be more abundantly .promoted. No such opportunity, however, has been afforded at this General Conference."

Thus, by the foregoing decision, has ceased for the present an agitation on this important point of Church policy which will eventually be reproduced and secure the end sought, though for the time being delayed. May the great Head of the Church by it bring glory to himself, and great good to all his people !

CHAPTER XVIII.

The Methodist Book Concern Forty Years Ago and Now.

THE entire valuation of this establishment in 1832 could not have much exceeded two hundred and fifty thousand dollars. Its history is of no small importance as con-nected with the literature of the Church. It was first established in the city of Philadelphia, in 1789, with a borrowed capital of six hundred dollars.

Rev. John Dickins, then the stationed min-ister in that city, was elected its first "Book Steward" and editor. The first book printed by the "Concern" was Wesley's edition of "à Kempis," a little devotional work by a "Ro-man Catholic." During his first year in office Mr. Dickins published "The Arminian Maga-zine," "The Methodist Discipline," "The Saints' Everlasting Rest," a "Hymn Book," and "Wes-ley's Primitive Physics."

It remained in Philadelphia until 1804, when

it was removed to Crosby-street, New York;
but by reason of its lack of funds, and its very
limited accommodations, its success was small
for a series of years. In 1828 it was placed
upon a more permanent financial basis, and its
business greatly enlarged. This was under the
supervision of Nathan Bangs, D.D., then editor
of the "Christian Advocate," and John Emory
and Beverly Waugh, Agents. The last two
named were afterward bishops in the Methodist
Episcopal Church.

Just forty years ago it was removed from
Crosby-street to Mulberry-street, where new
and more commodious buildings had just been
erected for its increasing business ; but in the
space of four years all was destined to be in
ashes. Its entire value at that time was estimated at not less than three hundred thousand
dollars, and the loss by fire at more than two
hundred and fifty thousand dollars. The report
of this fearful fire produced a most painful sen-
sation in all directions. Indeed, the news of the
sad conflagration was carried by the winds of
heaven. A leaf of a Bible was picked up in
Brooklyn, three miles away from the smoking
ruins, while the flames were yet raging, on
which were found these words : " Our holy and
beautiful house, where our fathers praised thee,

is burned with fire, and all our pleasant things laid waste." Isa. lxiv, 11.

The people sympathized with the Church in this sad disaster, and in a short time contributed nearly one hundred thousand dollars to repair the loss, by which the Agents were enabled to go on with their publishing interests.

· THE WESTERN BOOK CONCERN

At Cincinnati was established in 1820, with a small capital, and forty years ago was doing a quite prosperous business in the enterprising western portion of Methodism ; but in 1844 a heavy draft was made on these comparatively young and struggling institutions by reason of the Southern secession, and the division of their funds consequent thereupon ; nevertheless our Book Concerns of New York and Cincinnati since the fire of 1836 have distributed among the annual conferences and to the Church, outside of their own business expenses, one million five hundred thousand dollars. All the profits are appropriated to Church purposes in such ways as the General Conference prescribes.

The Agents now publish some two thousand different volumes of books and one thousand tracts.

The value of the real estate owned by the Concern in New York is shown by the following extract from the official report of the Agents to the General Conference of 1872 :

" At the last General Conference a commission was appointed with power to expend any sum not exceeding one million dollars ($1,000,000) in the purchase of real estate for the use of the Book Concern, Missionary Society, and other connectional institutions in the city of New York, and to raise the money by loan or otherwise.

" In accordance with this authority, the said commission, in the spring of 1869, purchased a property on the corner of Broadway and Eleventh-street at a cost of nine hundred thousand dollars, ($900,000,) three fourths (¾) of which is owned by the Book Concern, and cost, including forty-two thousand nine hundred and four dollars and thirteen cents ($42,904 13) for finishing and fitting up for use, seven hundred and seventeen thousand nine hundred and four dollars and thirteen cents, ($717,904 13.) The other one fourth (¼) is owned by the Missionary Society of the Methodist Episcopal Church, and cost, when completed and ready for use, two hundred and thirty-two thousand four hundred and fifty-two dollars and forty-nine cents, ($232,452 49,) making the total cost of the building and lots nine hundred and fifty thousand three hundred and fifty-six dollars and sixty-two cents, ($950,356 62.)

"After reserving sufficient space for Book Concern, Missionary Society, and other connectional purposes—such as rooms for wholesaling and retailing books and periodicals, mailing department, library room, bishops' room, board room or chapel, agents, editors, and missionary secretaries' offices, etc.—there remained a large portion of the building unoccupied for Church or benevolent purposes, which is rented to several parties for an annual rent of seventy-two thousand seven hundred dollars, ($72,700,) which will pay the interest at seven per cent. per annum on the whole cost of the property, nine hundred and fifty thousand three hundred and fifty-six dollars and sixty-two cents, ($950,356 62,) being sixty-six thousand five hundred and twenty-four dollars and ninety-six cents, ($66,524 96,) and leave a balance of six thousand one hundred and seventy-five dollars and four cents ($6,175 04) toward paying the taxes and insurance.

"By the said commission the Agents were authorized to issue bonds for five hundred thousand dollars, ($500,000,) payable after three years, and due in fifteen years from June 1,

1869, for part payment of the above-named property. These bonds were all taken at par and accrued interest, without paying a single dollar for advertising or brokerage.

" The real estate at 200 Mulberry-street and Mott-street is used for manufacturing purposes, with the exception of a small portion, which is rented for eighteen hundred dollars ($1,800) per annum."

THE CIRCUIT PREACHERS WERE THE "BOOK AGENTS" FORTY YEARS AGO

For selling the books of. the establishment as they traveled their circuits, and the presiding elders were expected to supply them with all they could sell. · Now we apply directly to our "Book Concern" or "Depository Agents" for them as they are needed.

THE REPUTATION OF OUR "BOOK CONCERN"

Until within a few years past has stood above reproach. There has not been till of late even a suspicion of dishonorable dealing in the financial management of its affairs ; but unhappily there have been created suspicions of " fraud and mismanagement" in the practical workings of some of its departments, which have had a somewhat damaging effect on its former good name.

Several investigations into the alleged "frauds

and mismanagement" had been made by the "Book Committee" before the session of the General Conference of the present year, but each investigation resulted in divided opinions with reference to the complaints referred to them, and, as a consequence, in majority and minority reports, with but little satisfaction to the committee or to the public.

Such was its condition when our recent General Conference met, to which the investigation of the whole affair legitimately belonged—the only tribunal which could give its official final decision of the merits or demerits regarding these allegations of "fraud and mismanagement."

To this tribunal the Church looked with the deepest solicitude. Many outside the Church had predicted that the scandal would not be properly exposed, nor the subject thoroughly investigated, by this our highest Church authority; but, to the great satisfaction of all the friends of the Church, and to the equally great disappointment of her enemies, a most thorough investigation was there determined upon and made.

A "special committee" of seventy-two was raised, two thirds of whom were lay delegates, thorough business men, for this purpose, who

15

made a most searching investigation into the charges and specifications brought before them. After a long and thorough examination into all these matters, they came to their decision with remarkable unanimity. Their report was adopted by the General Conference without discussion, and with scarce a dissenting voice. Because of its importance, notwithstanding its length, we give it entire, as follows : ˎ

REPORT OF THE SPECIAL COMMITTEE ON THE AFFAIRS OF THE BOOK CONCERN IN NEW YORK.

" *To the General Conference of the Methodist Episcopal Church now in session:* Your special committee, charged with the investigation of alleged frauds and irregularities in the management of the Methodist Book Concern at New York, beg leave to report:

" That they have had the matters referred to them under consideration, and have made as thorough and searching an investigation as the limited time allowed would permit.

" The committee was organized by the election of B. R. Bonner, of St. Louis, as Chairman, and A. D. Wilbor, of Genesee Conference, as Secretary.

" After deliberation, the committee adopted

as *Rules of Order and Proceeding*, and as questions to be investigated and voted upon, the following, to wit:

" I. Any member of the committee proposing to call for the production and examination of persons or papers shall make such request in writing, and in such request shall specify such persons or papers, and shall point out especially the facts which he designs to establish or disprove by such persons or papers;

" *Provided*, That the persons and papers brought before the committee may be used for any purpose that may throw light upon any matter within the jurisdiction of the committee.

" II. The hearing of the facts, evidence, testimony and explanation shall be before the whole committee in open session, at which every member is expected to be present.

" III. Members of the committee shall not express opinions on the merits of the case or the proofs offered during the hearing. But each member shall be at liberty to ask any relevant questions he may think proper and necessary to a full understanding of the subject.

" IV. After the proofs and explanations are all submitted, the committee shall alone, with closed doors, proceed in their order to consider and vote upon the following questions, namely:

"*Question* 1. Have frauds been practiced in the printing, bindery, or any other department, by which the Book Concern has sustained loss? If so, by whom? How much loss was sustained? At what time or times were said frauds committed?

"*Q.* 2. Have there been any irregularities in the management of the business of the Concern, by which losses have been, or might have been, sustained?

"*Q.* 3. Have losses, if any, been of such magnitude as to endanger the financial strength of the Concern, or to materially impair its capital?

"*Q.* 4. Were the business methods of the departments such as to afford opportunities for frauds and peculations by subordinates? And is it reasonable to presume that such frauds, [or peculations,] if committed, could have been prevented by the enforcement of more thorough and business-like methods?

"*Q.* 5. Are there reasonable grounds to presume that any Agent or Assistant Agent is, or has been, implicated or interested in any frauds that may have been practiced on the Concern?

"*Q.* 6. Are the present methods of accounts

and modes of conducting the business such as to insure reasonable and ordinary protection against frauds and irregularities?

" *Q. 7.* Is the report of the Agents to this General Conference a fair exhibit of the assets and liabilities of the Concern?

" V. After a vote has been taken on each of the foregoing questions, any member of the Committee may propose any other question in writing, which the committee, by a vote, may entertain and order to be voted upon.

"VI. After the separate vote has been taken on each question, a report shall be drawn up embodying the judgment of the committee as thus rendered, with such expressions as may be deemed proper in relation to the same.

"VII. The specific statements of charges in Dr. Lanahan's report to the General Conference shall be taken up and examined in their order as numbered.

" The more expeditiously and thoroughly to investigate the several matters referred to us, consisting of the *majority* and *minority* reports of the Book Committee, and the testimony therein referred to; the statements and exhibits of Drs. Carlton and Lanahan; with the reports of the several accountants who have examined the affairs of the Book Concern, your committee ordered and appointed the following sub-committee, to wit:

" 1. A committee, composed of John Evans, Colorado, W. H. H. Beadle, Des Moines, and J. B. Quigg, Wilmington, to collate and report to us, first, the points of agreement; second, the points of disagreement in the majority and minority reports of the Book Committee.

" 2. A committee, consisting of John Owen, Detroit, J. C. M'Intosh, S. E. Indiana, and W. H. Olin, Wyoming, to collate and report the points of agreement and disagreement in the reports of Messrs. Kilbreth and Gunn, the experts employed by the Book Committee and Dr. Carlton; also, to examine the books of the Book Concern as to their past and present condition.

" 3. A committee, consisting of John Evans, Colorado, A. Bradley, Pittsburgh, J. B. Quigg, Wilmington, to examine and report upon the charges of fraud and irregularities in Dr. Lanahan's report (pages 17 to 21, inclusive—statements one to five) upon the question of frauds in the Printing Department.

" 4. A committee, consisting of D. N. Cooley, Iowa, William Deering, Maine, and W. J. Moses, Central New York, upon the charges of fraud and irregularities in the Binding Department, including statements six to seven, inclusive—pages 21 to 24—of Dr. Lanahan's report.

" 5. A committee, consisting of John Owen, Detroit, J. C. M'Intosh, S. E. Indiana, ·and W. H. Olin, Wyoming, to examine statements twelve to seventeen inclusive, of Dr. Lanahan's report as to fraud in *making false reports* of amounts of material used and the work turned out from the Binding Department.

"6. Also, a committee of three, consisting of L. J. Critchfield, Ohio, J. B. M'Cullough, Philadelphia, G. F. Gavitt, Providence, to examine the evidence in relation to statements eighteen, nineteen, and twenty in Dr. Lanahan's report, charging false entries in the books of the Book Concern.

"7. Also, a committee, consisting of W. H. H. Beadle, Des Moines, C. R. Brown, Michigan, and A. Bradley, Nebraska, to examine and report upon all the facts in relation to the publications of the several experts.

"After all the sub-committees had made the examinations practicable in the time at their disposal, and had submitted their several reports in writing to the special committee, and the several members of said committees had been questioned before the whole committee as to the evidence examined, and the facts found by them, and after hearing the other evidence before the committee, your committee, pursuant to its rules of order, went into private session with closed doors to consider and discuss the said several questions raised in the charges preferred and the questions proposed to be considered and voted upon.

"There were present at roll-call at this private session fifty-nine of the special committee, which was about the average number who have been present and examined said case during our sittings.

"Thereupon we proceeded to vote upon the questions as per order of proceedings above quoted, to wit:

" 1. On the first clause of *Question* 1, ' Have frauds been practiced in the Printing Department ?' the question was decided in the negative, ayes 7, noes 50.

" 2. On a vote on the second clause of said question, ' Have frauds been practiced in the Bindery by which the Book Concern has sustained loss ?' it was decided in the affirmative by a vote of ayes 49, noes 6.

" 3. On a vote on the third clause of said question, ' Have frauds been practiced in any other department by which the Concern has sustained loss?' the question was decided in the negative by a vote of ayes 7, noes 47.

"4. *Q*. 2. 'Have there been any irregularities in the management of the business of the Concern by which losses have been, or might have been, sustained?' was decided in the affirmative by a vote of ayes 46, noes 7.

"5. *Q*. 3. 'Have losses, if any, been of such magnitude as to endanger the financial strength of the Concern, or to materially impair its capital?' was decided in the negative by a vote of ayes 3, noes 48.

"6. *Q*. 4. 'Were the business methods of the departments such as to afford opportunities for frauds and peculations by subordinates?' The first clause of the question, as above quoted, was decided in the affirmative, ayes 49, noes 1.

"7. The second clause, to wit, 'Is it reasonable to presume that such frauds or peculations, if committed, could have been prevented by the enforcement of more thorough and business-like methods?'

"This also was decided in the affirmative by a vote of ayes 31, noes 20.

"8. *Q*. 5. 'Are there reasonable grounds to presume that any Agent or Assistant Agent is or has been implicated or interested in any frauds that may have been practiced in the Concern?'

"This question was decided in the negative, one only voting in the affirmative.

"9. *Q*. 6. 'Are the present methods of accounts and modes of conducting the business such as to insure reasonable and ordinary protection against frauds and irregularities?'

"This was decided in the affirmative by a vote of ayes 42, noes 12.

"10. *Q*. 7. 'Is the report of the Agents to this General Conference a fair exhibit of the assets and liabilities of the Concern?' was decided in the affirmative by the following vote: ayes 44, noes 3.

"Your committee, therefore, after as careful an examination of all the evidence at hand bearing upon the subject submitted to us as it has been possible for us in the time at our disposal to give to it, arrive at the conclusion that repeated frauds have been practiced upon the Book Concern.

"These frauds are found in the manufacturing department, and are located chiefly, if not wholly, in the bindery. Mr. Hoffman was superintendent of this department at the time of the perpetration of these frauds, and the evidence indicates that for a series of years he carried on a system of frauds by which the Concern sustained very considerable losses, the amount of which it is impossible to indicate with accuracy.

" 1. We are of the opinion that the business methods of this department were formerly such as to afford opportunities for frauds and peculations by subordinates, which these investigations show have been taken advantage of.

" 2. Your committee concur with Mr. Kilbreth in the statement made by him in his report before us, in which he says that 'in former years it is apparent that there was a great lack of system in the business transactions of the house, as shown on the books, and a great deal of confusion and careless book-keeping ;' as also in his further statement, that 'the business entries of the years 1862 and 1864, including also the bindery and periodical account of 1861, are totally inexcusable as specimens of accounts.'

" 3. Your committee also find that the losses sustained by frauds and irregularities are not of such magnitude as to endanger the financial strength of the Book Concern, nor to materially impair its capital.

" 4. That there are no reasonable grounds or proofs to justify an assumption that any Agent or Assistant Agent is or has been implicated or interested in any frauds which have been practiced on the Book Concern.

" 5. That the present method of accounts and modes of conducting the business are such as to insure reasonable and ordinary protection against frauds and irregularities, yet they are not altogether perfect.

" 6. In reference to the purchasing of paper through Mr. James F. Porter, we concur with Mr. Kilbreth, ' that under all the circumstances of the case we unhesitatingly regard it as a decided business impropriety.'

" 7. We deem it proper to refer to the transaction of the Book Concern with Messrs. Brown Bros. and Co., (see Mr. Kilbreth's Report, page 48,) because it was an unauthorized use of the credit of the Book Concern for the benefit of outside parties ; and although there was in this case no loss to the Book Concern, and we may reasonably believe the motives which prompted to the act were to promote the interests of the Concern, and to accommodate the Missionary Society of the Methodist Episcopal Church, South, yet to guard against its influence as a precedent we call your attention to it as an error fraught with peril to the interests of the Book Concern which should not be sanctioned.

" 8. As to question seven, submitted for our

consideration, whether the report of the Agents for 1871 ' is a fair exhibit of the assets and liabilities of the Concern,' we report that no testimony was introduced before the whole committee on that subject, though several members of the committee examined such evidence at the Book Room as was available. As the exhibit is made up in parts of estimated values of real estate and other property belonging to the Concern, such estimates must depend largely for their reliability upon the good judgment of the persons making up such exhibit.

"It is perhaps sufficient to say that your committee have no evidence before them tending to show that the exhibits should be different from what they are.

" Appreciating the important duties devolved upon us, and with an earnest desire to reach just conclusions, your committee have labored earnestly to discover the facts involved, and arrive at just conclusions embraced within the scope of the authority conferred upon us. We submit the foregoing as a summary of our conclusions.

" All of which is respectfully submitted.

" On the question of the adoption of the foregoing report as a whole by your committee, the same was adopted *unanimously* by a rising vote."

The character of that committee, the thoroughness of their investigation, and the result of their conclusions, are well expressed in "Zion's Herald" of June 13th by the editor, who was a member of the General Conference, and now one of the bishops of our Church, under the heading,

WHAT THE GENERAL CONFERENCE DID.

"The most important of the sessions of this body has concluded its work. Five weeks to a day it sat, patiently engaged in the work of the Church. Matters of the gravest importance came before it. The Church and the country had been tossed on a rough sea of controversy over one of her publishing houses. The waves of dispute were very angry, and ran very high. Elections of the gravest character came upon it. The settlement of wider matters, relating to Church interests at home and abroad, was also appointed unto it. Especially notable was it for the presence, for the first time, of laymen in its councils. Its work is done. What is that work? First, that which was first in the public and ecclesiastical mind, the New York Book Room troubles, were settled, to the peace of the whole community. A body of seventy-two members, two thirds and over laymen, was especially assigned to this case. That body divided itself into minute committees, and every particle of the voluminous evidence taken in all the previous investigations was carefully read. Besides this, much other testimony was received. We doubt if ever a subject was more thoroughly searched into, under the limitations of time that were necessarily imposed upon them. They could only have surpassed it by sitting as a commission after the adjournment of the Conference. That committee was presided over by a leading banker of St. Louis, Mr. Bonner, and had among its members superior men of busi- ness and brains, such as Hon. Wm. Deering, F. A. Gavitt, Esq., Rev. Dr. Thayer, Hon. Senator Lane, of Indiana ; Judge Price, of Iowa ; Gov. Dillingham, of Vermont ; Judge Goodrich, of Chicago ; Hon. John Owen, State Treasurer of Michigan ; Gov. Evans, of Colorado ; Rev. W. H. Olin, of Wyoming, a bred lawyer ; Judge Woodward, of Washington, and many others of like sort. Their report, unanimously adopted, sustained the main lines of complaint, and justified the efforts made to improve the *status* of affairs at New York. Yet it was so couched that no reflection came on the integrity of any of the officers of the Church. This result answered all the charges with which some of the press have been laden, that the scandal would not be exposed or suppressed. The Church did the square thing, and no one, unless determined to find fault, can complain of the manner in which this matter has been considered and adjusted. The General Conference completed this work by adopting the report with almost entire unanimity, and by placing entirely new men in both the Concern and the Committee, an act which did not reflect on the previous members, but simply said it is best to have a new order of things all through, so that every thing may start afresh and aright. The brethren selected as agents are able men. Dr. Nelson is a thorough business man, having successfully conducted the affairs of a flourishing seminary for many years in Pennsylvania. He is of rare agreeableness of manners, the soul of courtesy and honor, without self-seeking, devoted to the enlargement and prosperity of this great interest of the Church.

" His associate, J. H. Phillips, Esq., has been the real head for many years of the house in Cincinnati. He was one of the secretaries of the Conference, and by his goodly presence, portly and pleasant, as well as by the zealous seconding of his handsome associate secretary, Judge Cooley, of Iowa, he won the place from the rival lay candidate, J. P. Magee. The latter was set in nomination for the West, and it is likely would have been successful had he consented to stand, for large numbers of that section declared they would have supported him, and it would have been a fine proof of our common brotherhood had they crossed the Concerns in this manner. But his instant and peremptory decline prevented that consummation.

" The committee has on it many men of ability, financial and otherwise. Messrs. Taft, North, and Ferry, at New York, and Shinkle, Kilbreth, and Bruehl, of Cincinnati, are the lay centers around whom the twelve district members, chiefly clerical, revolve. Their character will insure business force, and their associates will give the needed literary completeness."

16

CHAPTER XIX.

Methodist Missions Then and Now.

IN the year 1832 the Missionary Society of the Methodist Episcopal Church had been in somewhat successful operation for thirteen years. It had then under its control several domestic but no foreign missions. These missions were in newly-settled parts of the country, among the white population, and in the feeble societies in the older sections, which for a time received aid from the funds of the society, but generally soon became self-supporting. Also there were established missions among the colored people of the South, both free and bond. It is to be regretted that separate statistics are not preserved of their numerical condition.

The colored members of the Church, bond and free, in all the twenty-two conferences, were reported for that year to be seventy-three thousand eight hundred and seventeen. These, of course, resided mostly in the South. Only a few of these belonged to the regular missionary appointments of that section of the Church.

There were also many missions among the Indians of the country. Of these, among the most prominent were our missions among the " Oneidas," the " Kansas," the " Choctaws," the " Cherokees," and the " Wyandottes." The last named attracted much attention. The manner of its origin was on this wise : John Stewart, a poor but pious colored brother of New York city, was strangely impressed, in the year 1816, to leave his home and travel due north-west to somewhere (of the distance or place he had no idea) and there preach the Gospel, which was designed for all people. These impressions his brethren regarded as visionary, and many sought to discourage him. But all in vain. He started on his journey, like Abraham of old, " not knowing whither he went," and guided, as he believed, by the divine Hand, he kept on his journey till he was constrained to stop, as he soon found, among the Wyandotte Indians, once a powerful nation, the most ancient settlers of both sides of the Detroit River. Here he made his mission known, and preached the "glorious Gospel " through an interpreter of his own race.

The word took effect. Soon God gave him many souls as seals of his divinely-appointed ministry. Poor John Stewart was soon the acknowledged "great apostle " of the Wyandotte

Indians. Of the fruits of this mission, among others, were Brothers " Between the Logs," "Bloody Eyes," "Striped Snake," "Monuncue," and "Gray Eyes," powerful chiefs of their nation, who became, in their way, eloquent and powerful Methodist preachers.

Other missionaries were in due time sent to them, and this mission was one of our most interesting and successful of any forty years ago. In the Minutes of that year, in all the Indian missions, there were reported 4,501 members.

In consequence of their unfortunate removal beyond the Mississippi they became somewhat disorganized, and the next year were reduced to 2,412, a decrease of 2,089.

During that year a new impetus was given to the cause of missions in our Church by the establishment of our first American Methodist Foreign Mission. This was the Liberia Mission in Africa. It began on this wise : Among those who had gone to reside in Africa from the United States were a few of our Church-members, people of color, and some colored local preachers of good standing and influence. These sent to the Parent Missionary Society a plea for help. The society heeded the call, and resolved to send them a missionary. Rev. Melville B. Cox, of the Maine Conference, offered to go. His offer was accepted, and he set sail October 6, 1832, for his important mission. His heart had been set upon Africa from the time of his appointment.

It is said that near the time of his departure for Africa his dear mother threw her maternal arms around his neck, and dropping her falling tears upon his face, exclaimed, " O, Melville, how can I give thee up?" When he, turning his imploring eyes toward Africa, exclaimed, " O, Africa, how can I give thee up?"

On the eve of his departure a friend asked him, " Mr. Cox, if you shall die in Africa, what would you have written on your tombstone?" His immediate reply was, " Though a thousand missionaries fall, yet shall Africa be redeemed." Another version of his answer is, " Though a thousand missionaries fall, yet let not Africa be given up." *

He reached his destination March 8, 1833, and with great enthusiasm entered upon the work of his mission, laying broad and specific plans for the future, and calling upon the Parent Society for additional means and missionaries to carry out his plans. But, alas! in a few brief months he was attacked with the African fever, and died July 21 of that year. Other mission-

* Bangs' "History of the Methodist Episcopal Church," vol. iv.

aries were sent, and the Liberia Mission has ever since been numbered among the most important in our foreign field. It now has an annual conference of somewhat more than twenty preachers, and a membership, including probationers, of more than two thousand, presided over by a resident bishop of African descent.

Another important mission was the Flat Head, or Oregon Mission. Its origin was calculated also to inspire enthusiasm for its support. The redmen of that forest region, as it then was, had become intensely interested to know more than was already known by them of the "white man's God" and the "white man's book." They therefore sent four of their principal men over the Rocky Mountains, a distance of three thousand miles, to St. Louis, to make the needed inquiries. Upon reaching their destination they promptly unfolded the object of their long wilderness journey.

Our Missionary Society immediately recognized it as a call from God, and responded to it by sending them two missionary preachers and a teacher, Jason and Daniel Lee, uncle and nephew, and Cyrus Shepherd. They went out with a large fur-trading company, and traveled from St. Louis, then on the borders of civilization, through forests and over mountains, for one hundred and forty-two days before they reached the Columbia River, the region of their destination. They immediately entered upon their laborious mission work, which for a time proved successful with the Flat Head tribes ; but these were destined in a few years to disappear, and in their place American enterprise and thrift were to supply the region with an intelligent, industrious, and numerous population, where now there is a prosperous State. Our Church has there now an annual conference of able ministers and a large and intelligent membership, a college and other schools, and an official weekly periodical, the " Oregon Christian Advocate."

These two missions of forty years ago awakened a much-needed interest, a zeal and liberality, in the Church, so that in the year 1834 the amount of receipts reached $35,700 15, more than twice the sum of the year before, which at that time was regarded as doing most nobly for this cause ; but it averaged only about six and a half cents per member for the whole Church.

In the New England conferences the average was nearly as follows : New Hampshire Conference, about four and one half cents per member ;

New England Conference, ten and three quarters cents ; Maine Conference, about sixteen cents per member. This last was a noble expression of the interest created by the appointment of their own beloved Cox to the Liberia Mission, and his early and lamented death.

WHAT A CONTRAST BETWEEN FORTY YEARS AGO AND NOW.

Besides the Liberia Mission Conference, to which I have just referred the reader, we have now the following foreign missions :

In China, that world of riches and glory, of superstition and idolatry, which had been till a few years past inaccessible to the Christian world, our Church has now a prosperous mission, which has been in progress since 1847. The Foochow Mission has 5 missionaries, 5 assistants, some 68 native preachers, and, including probationers, nearly 1,700 members. They have a printing-press, printing annually four million pages for the use of the mission, a female academy, and mission property valued at not less than $50,000.

Another mission field was opened in Kiukiang in 1868 with good results, and another in Peking in 1869, both of which are represented as giving signs of great promise to the Church.

Our German Foreign Mission had in 1871 an annual conference of 53 missionaries, 28 local preachers, 14 supplies in the regular work, and nearly 7,500 lay members, including probationers ; 36 churches, valued at $296,993 ; 25 parsonages, valued at $12,000, and more than 9,000 Sunday-school scholars.

The mission is thoroughly organized. It has a theological seminary, and other educational advantages. By the powerful influence of native German preachers, and that of the wonderful work of God among their American German brethren, it is destined to accomplish incalculable good to the people of that "fatherland." It was established only twenty-three years ago.

Our Scandinavian Mission had in 1871 13 missionary preachers, 25 local preachers, 3,662 members, 14 chapels, and 2,626 Sunday-school scholars. The missionary report of last year says, " Peace, love, and harmony reign in all the societies ;" and that " they are gaining more and more the respect and favor of the community generally." This mission has existed only eighteen years.

Our India Mission has an annual conference of 29 missionary preachers, 23 assistants, and

and 32 helpers; between 1,200 and 1,300 members, embracing those on probation; and of officers, teachers, and scholars in Sunday-schools about 2,000. "A great and effectual door is opened unto" the Church in this far-off land, and God is graciously giving the mission great success. This is the result of sixteen years' labor. . .

We have also missions in Bulgaria, in Italy, and in South America, which are doing good service in extending the kingdom of Christ in the earth. ·

Another important foreign mission field has been recently opened to Protestantism in the Republic of Mexico, for which, in the providence of God, American Churches must take special care. To this new opening our Church has very properly turned her attention, and appointed to its superintendency the Rev. Dr. Butler, the recent efficient superintendent of our missions in India, with an appropriation of ten thousand dollars; and what is also especially encouraging, she has decided to establish another forthwith in Japan, and appropriated twenty-five thousand dollars to the enterprise.

Let the Church rejoice in these new movements along the line of progress. ·

METHODIST DOMESTIC MISSIONS.

Our Domestic Indian Missions have been subjected to the embarrassing influences of the removal of the Indians to new homes beyond the Mississippi, to their constant numerical decrease, and to their wandering habits ; but still great good has been done among them through missionary efforts.

We have now 16 missionaries, 1,675 members, and 22 local preachers. This is a diminution in forty years in numbers of 2,829. "Lo, the poor Indian !" What a doomed race ! Nevertheless in the Oneida, the St. Regis, the Cattaraugus, the Alleghany, the Tonawanda, the Simcoe, and the Siletz Indian tribes our missionaries are "gathering fruit unto eternal life." In some of these they are "making marvelous advancement in agriculture, civilization, and an earnest religious life." In all "the Gospel is" seen to be "the power of God unto salvation" from sin unto many of these wandering natives of the forest.

In our German Domestic Missions there are 380 effective traveling preachers, nearly half of whom are wholly supported by their own people ; the others are supported in whole or in part by the Missionary Society. They have

476 churches, valued at $1,555,700. They report 210 parsonages, valued at $272,050, and raised for missions $19,056 50. Their membership is reported at 31,696, including probationers.* All this is the work of less than forty years.

The rapidity of German emigration to our country may be seen by the following facts : In New York city alone in nine years, including 1871, there came over from the "fatherland" 757,885 Germans. In the year 1871, 83,601, an increase over the previous year of 12,329.†

The Scandinavian Domestic Mission in 1871 had 42 missionaries, 151 local preachers, 56 churches, valued at nearly $120,000 ; and 20 parsonages, valued at about $21,500. They contributed to the funds of the missionary treasury more than $2,400. Six of the above stations are self-supporting. "This department of our missionary work is, like our German, alive all over." The tide of emigration from Scandinavia has swollen from 3,188 in 1863, to 16,668 in 1870. This mission began its operations twenty-seven years ago.

The Chinese Domestic Mission is a new one,

* See German correspondent in General Conference "Daily Advocate."
† See Report of Missionary Society for 1871.

and of vast importance to the Church and the country, in view of the rush of emigrants to our country from the celestial empire. It was commenced five years ago, and had in 1871 two missionaries in the field. It must eventually prove successful.

The Utah Mission is another of very recent origin. It had 6 missionaries in 1871, and 120 members, 3 Sunday-schools, 10 teachers, and 400 scholars. Its church property was then valued at $30,000. This mission is a peculiar one, and difficult yet with faith in God it must and will succeed. It is destined to become a great power in that Mormon land to counteract the false and iniquitous system there sanctioned. They raised last year for missionary purposes the sum of $9,000, which was expended in Utah. They call for more missionaries, and the Missionary Society of our Church is making ample provision for them, and our appointing power is supplying the men as fast as possible.

Another domestic territorial mission, commenced last year, is in Montana, a mountainous, sparsely settled region of the great Northwest. It is, however, a hopeful field, where in due time an abundant harvest will be gathered into the garner of the Lord. As yet their statistics are incomplete.

The last report gives 3 missionaries, 3 local
preachers, 50 members, 11 Sunday-schools, and
400 teachers and scholars.

In addition to these we have domestic mission work among the freedmen, extending
through all the Southern States. These freedmen show great eagerness to acquire knowledge,
and are fast rising into social and civil favor.
Many of them acquire property rapidly.

The membership of our Church is fast increasing among them ; but as the " Freedmen's
Aid " and " Church Extension " Societies have
these benevolent operations under their more
immediate supervision, their statistics are not
given in our missionary report. But the whole
work is, nevertheless, really missionary in its
character, and is meeting with glorious success.

We have domestic missions among our En-
glish-speaking population, and those of other
languages among us, requiring more money for
their support than all we send abroad for the ·
support of our foreign work. Our Missionary
Society recognizes this demand, and to its utmost extent provides for it. Wise men in and
out of our Church approve of the effort to
Christianize all classes of the people in our
country.

OUR AVERAGE CONTRIBUTIONS PER MEMBER.

Forty years ago, as before stated, the average contributions per member were only some six and a half cents. Our contributions in 1872 from all sources amounted to $661,000, which, when averaged among all our ministers and lay members, give us an average of a little less than forty-seven cents per member. This average, though far less than what it should be, is an increase quite creditable to our Church, especially when we consider the number of collections and subscriptions taken in a conference year for various benevolent objects. Not less than seven or eight others are ordered by our General Conference. Two of these, " The Freedmen's Aid " and the " Church Extension " Societies, are closely allied to the cause of missions. If these were added they would swell the amount of our benevolent contributions for real missionary purposes to a much higher figure.

The Church, however, ought to average at least one dollar per member for the mission cause alone. It is worthy of it. The open fields throughout the world are ripe for the harvest. In those countries where papacy has kept out the truth for centuries the Christian Church can now enter and reap down the whitening harvest. All Europe, all Asia, all America, and, indeed, the whole world, is open to the spread of Gospel truth as never before.

The call is loud to the Church to enter these open fields and "gather fruit unto life eternal." Where is there an enlightened Christian in the whole Church who does not feel his "heart burn within him" *to do all he can* to extend "this Gospel of the kingdom throughout the world?"

Part Second.

METHODISM: PRESENT AND PROSPECTIVE.

———•———

THE writer of the foregoing pages has made frequent reference to our past successful progress and present prosperity as a Church, and taken a hopeful forward look toward great and increasing success for years to come.

But we must not be forgetful of the contingencies which must be met on the part of his Church, with fidelity to the cause of God and in constant harmony with the claims of an all-wise and gracious Providence and of human agency.

We call the careful and prayerful attention of our ministers and lay members to some of the various demands upon us which are inseparably connected with our present and future welfare as a Church, as suggested in the following chapters.

17

CHAPTER I.

Methodism—Her Dangers and Her Duties.

———•———

THE present numerical strength, financial ability, excellent system of doctrine, efficient Church polity, great .educational facilities, and other favorable denominational characteristics of Methodism, whether taken singly or collectively, give a hopeful look for future success. We are prone to think that her borders are so widely extended, that her stakes are so firmly set, that her " mountain " is so " strong," and her " walls " so impregnable, that there can be no chance of a failure to fulfill the great mission for which God in his providence has raised her up. But thoughtful minds see the need of great care and caution lest her power for good be turned into wrong channels, and she fail of the end sought—" the spread of scriptural holiness over all lands."

Paradoxical as it may seem, her success may prove her failure, her prosperity her adversity, and her triumphs her overthrow. We should take good heed that we be not found bowing the knee and offering idolatrous worship to this *beau ideal* of Methodistic greatness and glory instead of paying the homage so appropriately due to Him who is "the author and finisher of our faith." Let us carefully consider some of the *dangers* and *duties* growing out of the past success and present prosperous condition of Methodism. We will, then, first state that

METHODISM, BY HER NUMERICAL STRENGTH, HAS HER SPECIAL DANGERS AND DUTIES.

In another chapter attention has been called to the fact that our Church has a million and a half of members. If her prosperity continues she must number many millions by the close of her second century. But her *real* strength is not to be found in her numbers. When other denominations of Christians had been long established and had become numerically strong, Methodism began, in the midst of great opposition and poverty, to outstrip in success these older and stronger Churches. By what means? "By the weapons of warfare which are not carnal, but mighty through God to the pulling down of the strongholds" of all opposing influences.

But what if her vitality should be lost, and she be left to boastfully count up her numbers to ascertain her real strength ? She would then offend God, as did David when " he numbered Israel." Gideon was stronger with his three hundred " valiant-hearted men," who could endure the severest tests, than with all the thirty-two thousand who first came to the conflict. Methodism, with all her numbers, if she come " not up .to thè help of the Lord " in her great mission, is liable to be " cursed mightily," as . was Meroz of old for a like failure of duty.

There is a fearful responsibility resting upon her. " The kingdom of darkness " yet extends over a vast majority of our fallen race. " There remains yet very much land to be possessed ; " and unless she properly cultivate her appropri- . ate part thereof, as our great Lord of the vineyard demands of her, a blighting curse will rest upon her for " cumbering the ground." May Methodism—" Christianity in earnest," as Dr. Chalmers called it—be enabled to put to useful and active service in her wide field each and all of her great membership, and " keep them at it, all at it, and always at it," for Christ's sake !

THERE ARE DANGERS AND DUTIES OF METHOD-
ISM, ALSO, IN RELATION TO HER FINANCIAL
PROSPERITY.

Our Church has risen from a state of extreme poverty to comparative affluence. This is not alike apparent in all parts of our extended borders. In the New Hampshire and some other New England Conferences we fail to secure it. In some parts of the South, devastated by the ravages of war, her members are mostly poor; and especially the recent bondmen, but now rejoicing freedmen, are yet in the low vale of poverty. So also are many of the new settlers of the far West struggling against financial embarrassments. But there are in various portions of Methodism, among its members, many who are in highly affluent circumstances, some of princely wealth, men capable of bestowing their money with a liberal hand upon our various Church enterprises if they are so disposed, and there are some noble examples among them of doing it. But there is a dangerous tendency on the part of rich men to use their means for what is not for the glory of God or the well-being of their fellow-men. We can see this tendency to lavish their money upon personal decorations, superfluous ornaments, unreasonably costly apparel, and extravagant style of life in general. Others bestow it very bountifully toward the erection and support of splendid and extravagantly-furnished church edifices; while others still *hold* and *hoard* their treasures with a miserly grasp for future days, and leave the cause of God to languish by their neglect. There is a proneness to trust in "uncertain riches." The Church may lose her vitality thereby, and, like the ancient Laodiceans, come to feel that she is "rich and increased in goods, and has need of nothing," in herself quite equal for all emergencies, when she is really poor and powerless by the lack of the "one thing" most needful—"the true riches."

"But I am persuaded better things" of most of her membership, "things that pertain to salvation," though I thus write of others and of the natural tendency of earthly riches. Much faithful instruction on the part of our religious teachers, and much earnest prayer, watchfulness, and "holy living" on the part of our clerical and lay membership, will be needed to carry into constant practical use the good old Wesleyan rule, to "*get* all you can, *give* all you can, and *keep* all you can;" that is, be industrious to *acquire*, frugal in expenditure, cheerful and liberal, according as God has prospered you, to *give* to all good causes, and then *save* the rest for providential necessities. To this end the wealth of each Church-member needs to be *consecrated* to God, together with all he is and all he has, and indeed is *already consecrated*, by each truly devoted disciple. For he who is faithful in the use of "this world's goods" can with greater safety be trusted with "the true riches" than he who wastes or hoards "his Lord's goods."

We can also most distinctly see that there are special dangers and duties with reference to our extensive

MISSIONARY ENTERPRISES.

The enthusiasm in our Church for the cause of missions began to be developed some forty years since, at which time our first foreign missions were established. It continued to grow with her growth, and to strengthen with her strength. until it reached its climax in 1861, at the time of the breaking out of the rebellion. Till then her treasury received, annually, increased funds, and it was confidently expected that before now her contributions would have reached to a million dollars or more. But, unfortunately, since then her zeal and her missionary receipts have been nearly at a stand-still, her contributions having been about the same from year to year.

This is not in keeping with her constant increase in numbers and wealth, nor is it in harmony with the new openings which are continually made, by the providence of God, for the spread of the Gospel in lands which until recently have been inaccessible to the Church of Christ. And, especially; it is not in accordance with the pressing demands for more men and means in the field she now occupies. There is need, to-day, of a revival of the old missionary fire, kindled by such burning eloquence as came from the hearts and fell from the lips of her former missionary secretaries— Dr. Pitman and Dr. Durbin—in their palmiest days, such an enthusiasm as shall burn into the *hearts* and open the *pockets* of our people to give "as God hath prospered them." Methodism is in danger of resting at ease at this point when God speaks, in language too plain and too distinct to be misunderstood, unto her to "go forward."

There is also danger that she will neglect the imperative demands of the foreign field by reason of the pressing needs of her domestic or home work. Not that there is too much done·at home. Far from it; she is not doing enough. But when the openings are so wide and the demands so great for the Gospel in lands where "the people sit in the darkness of nature's night," it must have a depressing influence upon all right-minded Christian people to feel that the larger portion of all our contributions never go to aid our foreign work. Could not more be raised, and raised easier, if our foreign and domestic mission work should be placed under the supervision of separate organizations? This question is now being seriously considered by some of the leading minds in the Church. In some way our contributions for both foreign and domestic uses ought to be greatly increased.

Another danger to our mission work is, the depressing influences and depleting effects of *overworking* our foreign missionaries. Some of our foreign missions *may* fail, some have *already* failed. Many of our most prosperous *are not*, and *never were*, adequately manned. For the want of more men and means our missionaries there are overworked by their laborious efforts to meet the pressing demands of their missions, and in their labors to extend their influence into the new openings around them.

While the Church prays "the Lord of the harvest to send more laborers into the harvest-field," she will also need to accompany her prayers with greatly increased contributions and corresponding effort to extend the Gospel among all mankind, in order to receive gracious answers to her prayers.

METHODISM HAS ALSO DANGERS AND DUTIES WITH REFERENCE TO THE REQUISITE QUALI- FICATIONS FOR HER MINISTRY.

In a previous chapter reference has been made to our seminaries, colleges, and theological schools, and to the good they have accomplished for the Church during the last forty years. What a *change* have we witnessed—a great and favorable change—in the opinions of our minis- try and membership on the subject of theolog- ical schools ! The prevailing sentiment of the Church may now be presumed to be in favor of the theological education of her ministry in such schools whenever practicable.

It would be an occasion of great joy to many of our people if our young men who are to enter our itinerant ministry could have the advantages of three years' academic study preparatory to entering college, then a full collegiate course of four years more, and then three years more in a theological seminary, before entering our trav- eling connection for their important life-work.

The more of such well-educated, divinely-called, and graciously-qualified ministers in our itinerant ranks the better for all concerned. With open hearts and arms the Church should welcome them.

But may the day be far distant when such *only* shall be admitted to our itinerant ranks ! Even the exclusion of all but graduates of colleges from our theological schools would prove a hazardous step. No less so would be the non-admission of all applicants for membership to our conferences who had never received their three years' training in some one of our theological schools.

God often calls to the Christian ministry men from on ship-board, from the work-shop, from the fishing-boat, and from the plow at such periods in their lives when it would be impracticable for them to spend even *three years* in a theological seminary before entering upon their divinely-called mission.

With good health, clear heads, pure hearts, ·industrious habits, careful self-culture, and, above all, with the power of the Holy Spirit, they make efficient ministers of the Gospel. Such were some of the men whom Christ called into his early ministry. Such were some of Wesley's very efficient helpers in the infancy of

Methodism. Such have been some of her leading ministers both in England and America during her history of a whole century and a third of another. Such are needed still in various parts of our widely-extended fields as well as college and theological graduates, who in their appropriate spheres of labor and influence will accomplish great good.

Our ministry should be spiritual, divinely called, and drawn from the people among whom they are to serve—men who know how to sympathize with "the common people" of their various pastoral charges; men who understand their peculiar tastes, their real necessities, their temptations, and their struggles with the adverse scenes of life. Such men are needed in the ministry every-where; and whether they graduate from the college, the theological seminary, or the work-shop, or any other common avocation of life, they know how to instruct the *heads* and touch the *hearts* of the middle and lower strata of mankind, which embrace the majority of all communities. Such hear Christ through his own chosen ministers more gladly than do the so-called higher grades of mankind.

Methodism has always been supplied and sustained mainly by people from the middle and lower walks of life—by those who have been

mentally, financially, socially, and morally elevated by her quickening and exalting influences.
If the cause of God, through her instrumentality,
is to go on as in the past, her ministry must be
educated (in order to real efficiency) in a manner which shall not *emasculate* their physical
energies, or render them too delicate to touch
the *rustic* part of the people, nor cause them to
be exalted above their business—an education
which will not create a " spirit of caste " among
their fellow-laborers, nor influence them to feel
that superior advantages entitle them to the
best stations.   Otherwise, whatever their education, they will become disqualified for the
ministry, *especially* the Methodist ministry.
They are mere *nuisances*, humbugs, not to be
tolerated by the people.   " True education,"
says a certain writer, " never lifts a man out
of his sphere, but renders him efficient in every
toil the cause of Christ may call him to."   We
should most heartily give thanks to the great
Head of the Church that our Methodist institutions of learning have very extensively produced
true, earnest men, who are willing, with hearts
· and hands, to work for Christ uncomplainingly
in any department of his great spiritual vineyard.
    In our solicitous forward look for Methodistic

success, we see the need of constant care to keep our ministry in the true " apostolic succession," called of God whether *learned* or *not,* and *qualified* by the Holy Ghost for their work, and true to our itinerant ministry.

There are other dangers and duties which might be appropriately referred to if time and space would justify ; but in the light of such as have been alluded to the common reader (if he has not already) may easily discern them, though they be not specially here named.

Whatever dangers there are to be avoided by Methodism may she timely and safely escape them, and perform all her duties promptly and faithfully, to the glory of God and the well-being of mankind !

CHAPTER II.

Methodism—Her Responsibilities with Reference to the Youth of our Country.

———•———

IN another place I have called attention to the numerical strength of Methodism, and stated that we have, as seen by our Church statistics, some one and a half million members, and that we may safely estimate that some four or five times this number are adherents of our denomination.

Is it not then safe to calculate that of this vast number there are some two or three millions of children and youth who are in their minority, and millions more cared for by no evangelical Church in particular, who are under the soul-destroying influences of infidelity, popery, and other forms of fatal error, many of whom are "led captive by Satan at his will?" Among these are vast numbers of poor outcasts, penniless beggars, neglected orphans, and children of dissolute parents, whose low habits, vitiated tastes, and neglected mental and moral culture, show most distinctly that "no man careth for their souls."

Our Church has a special responsibility resting upon her to look after the present and eternal welfare of all these millions of youth. She should send forth her servants into all "the highways and byways," not only after adults, but all the children and young people, and invite them to the means of grace, that our "houses may be filled," and others erected constantly. She has most excellent facilities for their improvement at this day above any former time, which she should eagerly take advantage of, and faithfully seek after all for whom the provision is or can be made.

Among these is our well-organized Sunday-School Union, with its thousands of library volumes, Sunday-School Advocate, Teachers' Journal, Sunday-School Requisites, and, to some extent, charity contributions, to aid poor and needy schools now existing, and, as far as possible, to establish mission schools in our country.

The work of systematic, organized canvassing of parishes each month by committees appointed to this special duty has been and is being successfully tried in some sections of our Church, and, in the estimation of good judges, is worthy of imitation by our people in many other parts of our great field.

Does not our blessed Lord and Master call upon his modern servants to go out into the streets and lanes of our cities, and into the highways of our country, and invite, yea, compel, if possible, by earnest entreaty, all grades of our neglected or wayward youth to come to our Sunday-schools and enjoy the " rich feasts " there provided ?

In a recent communication in " Zion's Herald," Bishop Haven says : " It is estimated that there are six millions of people in the United States who are denominationally connected with the Methodist Church ; there are enrolled in our Sunday-schools about a million and a quarter. Or, in other words, only one in five of our people are connected with our Sunday-schools. The facts thus presented demand the careful consideration of every Christian. Undoubtedly we may throw out of the account a million and a half who are too young, or infirm, or sick, or caring for the sick, or otherwise excused from attending the Sunday-school, but even then we have two millions and a quarter unaccounted for. No one can claim that more than a million should be excused, and that leaves a million and a quarter who ought to be in the Sunday-schools of our Church. Many of these are young people who have attended more or less, and for some reason have dropped away, and are drifting off from the old ways, and incurring danger of fatal shipwreck. Many more are members of the Church, who have no good excuse for their non-attendance. They need to study the word of God, for they have all too little knowledge of its precious truths, and certainly they owe it to the Church, and to the young, and to those who are toiling in this field of labor, that they as Christians should give this all-important interest and institution of the Church the support of their presence, sympathy, and active effort.

" The General Conference which has just closed has given special attention to the cause of Sunday-schools. It has placed at the head of this department a man who stands confessedly at the head of all workers in this branch of Christian effort—a man well known and tried— and under his management there is no reason why the inexcusably absent million and a quarter may not be brought in. It can be done, and it will be done if our ministers and Sunday-school officers, teachers, and scholars will work. Work is the word, and enough of it, with God's blessing, will double the Sunday-schools of our Church within the next four years."

Our Church has also advantages for the education of our youth in her many institutions of learning in the country open for their benefit, and to which they are or should be cordially invited. These schools are favorably located in different States and conferences, and thus made easily accessible to the multitudes, who need the mental and moral culture they can impart. Many more such institutions will be needed and established for the increasing demands which our future progress will make imperative upon our people. There is present ability in the Methodist Church to richly endow our existing institutions, and even establish more if the wealth of our people can be turned into the right channels. Rich men abound in the Church ; but the manifest tendency now is, as before stated, to turn this wealth too freely, as compared with other wants, into extravagant personal and family expenditures and costly churches, while our institutions of learning, in some instances at least, are left to languish for want of funds. This tendency in the use of moneyed wealth, it is believed, is destined to be changed to more liberal bestowment upon our educational interests. Some noble examples have already been witnessed among our people of rich men who have consecrated largely of

their wealth to aid these important objects, and
others will follow in their path. Our pastors,
our periodicals, and noble-hearted laymen will
call attention to this channel of benevolence
and·usefulness, and we shall see our schools
better cared for.

The demand for the education of our youth
is constantly increasing. We need educated
Christian young gentlemen and ladies for clerks
in our counting-rooms, for teachers in our academies and high and common schools, for editors
and authórs, for Sunday-school superintendents
and teachers, for ministers in the home and mission fields of the Church, and many other departments of business life. They, indeed, are needed
every-where, not to the exclusion of the less
educated, for there is room for all to work somewhere in the·Master's great vineyard ; but educated youth, with the love of God in their souls,
can be made more available for, and better
adapted to, any and every place than they otherwise could be. The Church should make
special efforts to rally our youth to our schools.
Even the low, degraded, and poor should not
be overlooked. They may be inspired to rally
their energies, and be made bright and shining
ornaments in the world.

There is a special responsibility resting upon

our Church to labor for the conversion and religious culture of the youth of our country, and
particularly for those who are more immediately
under her influence. Her decline or continued
growth depends largely upon it. The welfare
of coming generations is involved in it. . The
present and eternal salvation of millions requires
it. Youth is the season when this special effort for their personal consecration to Christ
and religious culture will prove most successful.

Earnest, believing prayer, united with corre-
spondingly faithful effort, *must* secure a gracious
harvest. They need the moral and religious
culture of Church and Sabbath-school instruction. They need the example and hallowing
influences of pious homes. They need all the
mental and moral discipline of the best schools
which can be possibly afforded them. But,
above all, they need *conversion* to Christ and the
cultivation of *Christian virtues*, short of which
all other culture will not avail them " in the day
of the Lord Jesus."

The Church should not stop short of this
saving result. If any of our youth should resist
all proper personal effort the responsibility must
rest on *them;* but faithful effort for their salvation must in a majority of cases prove successful. Such " labor shall not be vain in the

Lord." It may not be one particular Sunday-school lesson, or sermon, or song of praise, or exhortation, or prayer, that will be the means alone in the salvation of a soul ; but *all these combined* should be employed to bring about such a happy result.. While a Paul plants and an Apollos waters, God giveth the increase.

The stars will, at last, be found in the right crowns when " the wise shall shine forth as the brightness of the firmament," and those who have " turned many to righteousness " shall shine with brighter effulgence, having these " stars for ever and ever " to bedeck " their crown of rejoicing."

CHAPTER III.

Methodism—Her Converts and Probationers.

———◆———

OUR Church began in a revival of religion, and her rapid increase has been kept up by an almost unbroken succession of revival efforts. Our fathers in this country, a half century ago, had remarkable revivals of religion, and gathered much precious " fruit unto life eternal ; " and other denominations of Christians made large accessions to their communions by securing many who were converted at our altars. Similar revival efforts at this day produce similar results. Our Church periodicals bring us, from week to week, cheering news from the different parts of our work of great and precious revivals, in which hundreds are converted to Christ. We live in days of great " refreshing from the presence of the Lord." Our denominational increase, though less rapid than fifty years ago, is, nevertheless, very encouraging to all the lovers of our Zion. But this increase is not in proportion to our reported revival success. This fact is so apparent that it is awakening in some of our most thoughtful and careful observers special attention. It is a matter which cannot be too carefully considered, and the causes well understood, and the remedies faithfully applied. .

The true Church is the bride of Christ and the mother of his spiritual children. For them she has " travailed in birth, till Christ has been formed in them." " They are her joy and crown," and she has " no greater joy than to know that they are walking in the truth." If true to her Lord and his cause, she will throw around them her arms of protection, and extend to them all proper nurturing care.

Different branches of the Church of Christ provide different methods for securing their converts to their own communions. Methodism offers special advantages to her converts. In addition to the common means of grace enjoyed by her and other Churches, she provides a six months' probation. Into this relation the young converts can very properly be *immediately* received, and thereby placed under the special watch-care and guidance of the pastor and his assistant, the class-leader, and enjoy the benefits of weekly attendance on class. But special care should be taken by her pastors and members to gather in all her converts. Other Churches are not backward to secure theirs to their own respective communions ; and they are praiseworthy for all appropriate efforts to this end.

All converts should find their own proper homes. Methodism must not intrude herself into fields not her own.to gather fruit for which she has bestowed no labor, and should as carefully " look to herself" that she lose not the things she has wrought, lest she fail of " her full reward." She needlessly loses many of her spiritual children by unreasonable delays as well as by indiscreet though well-meant efforts in their behalf, thus causing Christ and his precious cause to be " wounded in the house of his friends."

It is also important that due attention be paid to the proper manner of this reception. The relation of a probationer with us is an important one. It involves special responsibilities. Lax administrators have been betrayed into injudicious methods of doing this part of their work. Some have been received into this relation in class without due form, explanation, or examination ; and others have been thus recognized not only without attention to these prerequisites, but without the knowledge of the class to which their names have been attached. Some, even, have had their names recorded as probationers without their own proper consent or knowledge, who, when interrogated by succeeding pastors, express surprise, and perhaps refuse to be thus recognized. By these loose methods of administration our Church has suffered the loss of many of her probationers. They have not felt the responsibilities of this new relation. To remedy this evil as far as possible more special care should be taken to impress them that they have, in this act, " taken the vows of God " upon them to be faithful to the end.

This should be done *openly* before the Church, when the pastor should give *full* and careful instruction and counsel in reference to the serious and permanent obligations which they then assume. But the chief cause of this loss is, doubtless, to be found in Christian families and in the Churches, by the lack of the Christian culture there required.

Young converts look for a hearty welcome into their new associations. They need this, as they break away from their former vain associations with the world. They need the special and earnest prayers of the Church. They need the hearty counsel, the cheerful co-operation, and faithful example of both pastor and people.

Says a judicious writer: "Scores die spiritually for lack of nurturing food and wholesome atmosphere in the Church. They are sometimes poisoned to death by the divisions in the Churches, or frozen to death by their coldness. Few spiritual 'babes' are lost where a Church is in a united and spiritual state, and when they are from the first carefully instructed, watched over, and introduced into such Christian services as their experience and talents render practicable."

Very few of our probationers will backslide or go from us to other Churches when we bestow on them proper care and suitable culture.

But with all this responsibility upon our Church toward her converts and probationers there is danger that these new recruits into her ranks may be left to feel that they can be carried on her shoulders or nursed in her lap without a proper sense of their own personal obligations, so that when they should have become strong men and women in Christ they will still remain weak, and become spiritually sickly, not capable of performing their appropriate work for the cause of God—a result of their own personal neglects, for which she cannot be held responsible. If they are advanced to full membership they seldom become efficient workers for Christ,

but generally remain dead-weights, mere hang-
ers-on — idlers in the vineyard of the Lord.
"We are persuaded better things of" most of
her young members—"things which pertain to
salvation," "though we thus speak." But we desire to call attention to the solemn responsibilities of their positions, that they may feel their
individual responsibility to act well their own
appropriate parts for Christ and his cause.

Every member of the Church, old or young,
is called upon to make known the blessedness
of the Gospel, and it seems to be the special
demand of the hour, with all the encourage-
ments which surround us, and the extent of the
Gospel field, all ripe for a golden harvest, that
the Church should become "thoroughly furnished unto every good word and work" by all
the aids within her reach, and use them to the
glory of God and the salvation of men. And
we may say with Paul, " Finally, brethren, whatsoever things are true, whatsoever things are
honest, whatsoever things are just, whatsoever
things are pure, whatsoever things are lovely,
and whatsoever things are of good report ;
if there be any virtue, if there be any praise,"
may our Church and all her spiritual children
" think on " and practically exemplify " these
things."

CHAPTER IV.

The Reciprocal Claims Upon Pastors and People Growing Out of Our Methodist Itinerant System.

HERE are reciprocal claims growing out of the relation of pastors and people, whether connected with our system of supplying pastors or the more settled ministry of other Churches. My aim is to show the reciprocal claims which must be met with cheerful fidelity to the cause of God in order to secure the continued success of Methodism. Among these I will name the following:

1. There should be mutual submission to the appointing power of the Church.

According to the established polity of our Church the itinerant pastor relinquishes the right of choosing his own parish. He entered the itinerant ministry with the express understanding that he would not enter into any negotiations with any people to become their pastor, but become pledged to keep himself free (while in the itinerant ranks, and able to do so) to go to any circuit or station required of him by the appointing power of the Church.

This is the rule. If any one's practice should vary from it, the stipulated engagement, into which he voluntarily entered, would be infringed, and, if adopted by our ministry extensively, would not only result in great embarrassment, but inevitable ruin to the itinerant system.

The itinerant has the right of reporting his embarrassments, of expressing his preferences, and stating his necessities to the proper authorities of the Church. This is perfectly reasonable, and in some cases really necessary; but he should never enter into any negotiations with any particular parish to become its pastor.

This duty of the pastor has its reciprocal claims on the part of the people of a station. They should never attempt any negotiations with certain select preachers, nor set up special demands for any particular one of them, to the rejection of others. The people of a station can and ought faithfully to represent their wants and wishes to the appointing power of the Church, and, if they choose, even petition for certain pastors, but ever yield cheerfully to the discretion of those who have the responsibility of making the appointments.

If the laity of our Churches or our congregations should ever become disloyal to our ap-- pointing authority our itinerant system must die. Our people should leave our noble itinerant plan, which has wrought such wonderful success during the past century, free to pursue its glorious mission untrammeled for all time to come.

2. Another duty growing out of our itinerant system is a reciprocal welcome by pastors and people.

The pastor, when appointed to a new station, should go cheerfully, joyously, and courageously to his work. What though his new field of labor may not have been his first choice, and not quite agreeable to his tastes? what though the Church may not be numerically, financially, or religiously strong and vigorous? yet he will find souls to save, and enough to do to tax all the energies of soul and body in the prosecution of his pulpit and pastoral work. And what a privilege to win souls to Christ in any place! Why should he not be cheerful, joyous, courageous? The Lord of the vineyard has said, " Lo, I am with you always, even to the end of the world."

A disheartened, discontented, murmuring pastor will soon diffuse his own spirit among his own people, and never will he do this more easily than when he first comes among them. He should be exceedingly careful at this point. I have known some to paralyze all their moral power for good among their people by entering upon their pastoral work in their new charges in a sad, complaining spirit.

This claim upon newly-appointed pastors has its corresponding claim on the part of the people of the stations to give them a hearty reception. What though they have just parted with a devoted minister, whom they loved most ardently ; what though he had been proved, in sickness and in health, to have been a friend of his people indeed ; what though they had sat under his ministrations with great delight ; has not the new pastor just left a beloved people, tried friends, and those with whom he had "taken sweet counsel ? " Has he not come among strangers "in weakness and fear and much trembling," to be criticised in all his movements ? He and his family will need to be more than human not to feel most keenly the greatly changed condition.

A hearty reception he greatly needs. It will · wonderfully cheer him on in his work and labor of love, and ever be held by him in grateful remembrance. And why not give him such a reception ? He professes to be the Lord's chosen messenger. He has been approved by the Church, and his character just indorsed by his conference. He comes to his new parish to comfort the sorrowing, to strengthen the weak, to visit the sick, to bury the dead. A cold reception must chill his soul, and work disastrously through all his term of service among them. Such sad results have been seen and felt again and again. I repeat, Let the people give their newly-appointed pastors hearty receptions !

3. There are also reciprocal claims with reference to removals and parsonages.

The Methodist pastor, for the sake of the Church, sacrifices the enjoyments of an established home. This, from the nature of his calling, he cannot provide for himself. Also, his furniture must be removed from place to place, marred, and deficient, and himself and family subjected to no small inconvenience and expense. The task of moving brings with it much hard labor, anxiety and perplexity, which few understand and fewer still appreciate. But these things are inseparably connected with the itinerant system, and must be heroically borne.

There are reciprocal claims belonging to the people of a parish, also, in these matters. They can lighten the burdens of these removals to a great extent, and are in duty bound to do it as far as possible. They should provide well-located, convenient and pleasant parsonages for their preachers, and keep them in good repair. They should provide at least all the needed heavy furniture, and see that every thing is in good condition for the reception and use of the family.

Where parsonages cannot be *built* nor *bought* for lack of funds, the stewards of the Church, in behalf of the people, should *hire*, and as far as· possible furnish, suitable houses ; and when thus provided, the pastors are bound to occupy and use them with all proper care, or provide for themselves without a murmur or unreasonable expense to the society they serve. ·

A pastor who is disposed to find fault with the house and furniture which his people have provided for him, when they have attempted to do well, will soon find he has given severe offense, and that his own influence is greatly harmed. When removals become unavoidable, the people of his station ought to lend a helping hand, by taking all reasonable burdens on themselves. And when they have done their best, there will still remain heavy burdens upon the removing pastor and family which no human aid can fully remedy. "Bear ye one another's burdens, and so fulfill the law of Christ."

4. We will now consider the reciprocal claims with reference to *salaries.*

The itinerant pastor is not expected to make any stipulated agreement with his people in regard to his salary. On going to his new appointment, it devolves upon the quarterly conference to decide upon this, according to what its members may regard as a fair estimate. The pastor will be obliged to grade his expenses accordingly.

There is a corresponding duty devolving upon the people of his parish through the quarterly conference, to place the estimate at a liberal and honorable figure. For "they who preach the Gospel should live of the Gospel," and surely "the laborer is worthy of his hire." This estimated salary should be placed high enough to remove the pastor from all reasonable anxiety with reference to current expenses, high enough with suitable economy to leave a small surplus in his hands at the end of the year to lay by for future want. When the estimate is thus settled upon, the people of the station, through the proper officers of the Church, should see to it that it is paid promptly—if possible monthly, at furthest quarterly, in advance. More than this. Substantial tokens of kind regard in presents to the pastor and family are good investments for the worthy receiver, but much better for the cheerful giver. For "it is more blessed to give than to receive." Some of us can testify to the blessedness of receiving, under such circumstances, and others who cheerfully give oft testify to the rich blessedness of so doing. With this liberal provision made for the pastor's support, it becomes his duty to devote all his time and talents to promote the religious welfare of his people. And why should he not devote himself wholly to this one work? To be "worthy of his hire" he must be a "laborer." To "live *of* the Gospel" he must "give himself wholly" *to* the Gospel; "never be unemployed, never triflingly employed, never spend more time at any place than is strictly necessary."

This is the disciplinary rule. If strictly lived up to the pastor will find no time to engage in worldly schemes for gain, none for jockeying in horses, none for any of those miserably penurious modes of trade which would waste time and degrade the minister. More than this. The itinerant pastor should rise far above all low, whining cant, all dolorous complaint about great sacrifices, small pay, poor stations, and pinching poverty, in order to excite sympathy. A whining, grumbling pastor is a perfect nuisance in any place, and at all times. He should either immediately reform, or retire from the ministry. If his pay is small, he should seek by faithful labors to show to the people that he deserves better fare. Should his parish prove to be undesirable, he should strive to make it better. Should he find his people to be poor, he should for the time being cheerfully share with them their poverty. But for the honor of the sacred office he should never disgrace his calling by descending to a whining cant, to low schemes for gain, nor by becoming a poor, whimpering beggar.

5. An early acquaintance should be mutually sought between pastor and people.

After becoming comfortably settled in his new home, the pastor's next work will be to cultivate a mutual acquaintance with his people. This will be found to be no easy task. The names, countenances, and places of residence being all new and strange to him, and the peculiar characteristics and circumstances of each being yet mainly unknown, the task will be difficult and sometimes quite embarrassing ; nevertheless, it must be undertaken without delay, and in due time accomplished.

In this peculiarly difficult but interesting work his mode of operations and social characteristics will be closely scrutinized.

He will need and must receive the sympathy and aid of his people in this work. They should make, early in the year, friendly calls at the parsonage, and thus seek an early acquaintance with its occupants. Some *shun* an acquaintance with the minister and family, and then complain bitterly of neglect. This is a great fault. If any wish an acquaintance why not show it ?

In his efforts to form an acquaintance early in the year the new pastor can be greatly aided by his people if they will take the time and pains to introduce him to friends, and even accompany him to different streets and neighborhoods for this specific purpose. The writer has been greatly assisted at different times by such timely efforts of kind friends.

Strangers coming into the parish should also seek an early introduction. Should they fail to do this, and still remain strangers to the pastor, they should blame *themselves*, not *him*, for the failure. I have known some who had even shunned an acquaintance and then complained of neglect, when they were utterly unknown to

the pastor. Why blame *him* when they are at
fault *themselves* in this matter ?

Again, it is the duty of the pastor to seek out
the weak, the wandering, the sick and afflicted
of his flock. This is imperative. He cannot
neglect them without becoming untrue to his
calling. For *apparent* neglect he will be liable
to censure, when the special cases demanding
attention will be unknown to him. To obviate
this difficulty those acquainted with special cases
demanding immediate attention should, in a
prudent · and judicious manner, inform him
thereof ; and a faithful pastor will take the first
opportunity to visit them.

While it may be perfectly appropriate for any
one to impart this information to the pastor, the
Discipline of our Church makes it specially oblig-
atory upon the *stewards* " to inform the preacher of any that are sick among them, or walk
disorderly, and will not be reproved ;" making
it evidently *their* duty to first visit the sick and
seek to win back the erring. A good suggestion this, by which our lay members should
practically profit more than they do. .

6. We will come now to another duty growing out of our itinerant system, for both pastors
and people. I refer to liberty of conscience in
political matters.

We live in days when great moral questions are stirring the public heart—when important issues are to be settled by political action—and as time passes on the great moral questions which must arise will assume more importance in the public mind, and must have significant bearings on political parties.

The itinerant minister will need to take some important part in these matters. He must read for himself the stirring events of the day. He will need to inform himself with reference to the great moral issues to be settled at the ballot-box.

By reason of his changing his pastoral relations every few years, and thus being thrown into new circumstances very often, he must learn that there is a time to speak and a time to be silent—a time to act and a time to refrain from acting; that while he should not ignore politics as a *science*, he should rise far above all party trammels, and act for himself *independently, prudently, conscientiously*, in his sphere, as a man and as a citizen.

There is a corresponding claim devolving on the people of his charge to leave him free to *speak* and *vote* according to the dictates of his own conscience, without friction, without censure, and without attempted trammels. More than this : the pastor, claiming this right for himself, should never attempt to dictate to his people in respect to their political action, nor censure them for their conscientious use of the elective franchise. ˙ Without this reciprocal free- dom between pastors and their people unprofit- able bickerings and untold evils will follow. With it peace and harmony, in this regard, will prevail in all our borders.

7. There are, also, reciprocal claims between pastors and people with reference to reputation . important to consider.

I regard every person's reputation of more importance than the choicest gold. When one resides long among old and tried friends his reputation may become so established as to be above reproach or even suspicion, and, there- fore, comparatively secure ; but if he shall be obliged to be often thrown into the midst of new surroundings and among strangers, to rise or fall according to the estimate of an untried public opinion, his case becomes essentially dif- ferent. Such is the condition of our itinerant ministers. Their people should " *hold them in reputation.*" Not *exalt* them above their place, up among the *stars*, nor *trample* them under their feet into the *dust*, but give them a fair and honorable place, just such as they are properly

entitled to by virtue of their calling as the
" under shepherds " of Christ, " the chief Shepherd " of all. They should be " esteemed very
highly in love for their work's sake." They
should " *be held*" there—neither too high nor
too low, but just where their talents and usefulness demand. This, with proper care and effort on the part of both people and pastor, can
and ought to be done. Speak well of them
and to them ; vindicate their characters when
assailed ; show them proper respect ; pray for
them. The people of each parish should do
this for their *own* sakes as well as for their pastor's, and especially for Christ's sake.

There is an equal claim on the pastors to
speak well of their people; to "hold" them "in
reputation also;" not magnify their faults, but
speak charitably of their foibles ; not report
them unfavorably abroad, but as far as possible
seek to encourage and promote " whatsoever
things are lovely, whatsoever things are true,
whatsoever things are of good report " at home
and abroad. The pastor may, unintentionally,
give a bad odor, and that very unjustly, to his
parish, by speaking very carelessly of some real
and many imaginary faults of his people—a
thing most scrupulously to be avoided.

8. There are many other reciprocal duties

growing out of our itinerant system, of which I might make mention, but have time and space for only one more. I refer to the duties connected with the close of the pastoral relation between minister and people in a given parish.

According to the economy of our itinerant system, this relation changes according to circumstances, once in one, two, or three ecclesiastical years. In his closing work in a charge the pastor has special duties to discharge. He must collect and arrange all the benevolent moneys ordered by his conference ; make his closing pastoral calls ; administer disciplinary rules in special cases of unworthy members ; review and make faithful records in the church books ; prepare a full and accurate " Pocket Register" for his successor, giving therein the names of members in full connection and those on trial—in separate columns—and their different streets and other localities ; also a list of subscribers to our various Church periodicals, and many other items too numerous here to name ; and then smooth the way for his successor to take his place with the least possible friction. Thus should the transition be made comparatively easy and pleasant. These are duties he owes not only to himself, but to his people and to his successor in office. From the neglect of it great harm may be done. It is feared that some pastors, during the last months of their term of service in their stations, while mingling with their people, make special effort to awaken sympathy in view of the coming event, by preaching exciting farewell sermons, and frequent needless allusions to their sadness in the expected separation. Thus the way is prepared, with weak minds, for great friction in the change soon to occur. This course is deserving of severe censure. Pastors should be discreet and faithful in all the closing work of their charges.

The people of the pastoral charge have their special duties also in this regard. They should promptly pay in all benevolent moneys pledged, cheerfully aid the pastor in his many closing labors, and smooth the way, as far as possible, for an easy transition to the next preacher.

These reciprocal duties, when faithfully observed in practice, will greatly strengthen the hands and encourage the hearts both of our ministry and membership, more closely unite them "in every good word and work," and make our Church more efficient than ever for the building up of the cause of Christ in the earth.

I will conclude this chapter with the appropriate words of Holy Writ, to both the pastors and laity.

Pastors ! " Feed the flock of God which is among you, taking the oversight thereof, not by constraint, but willingly; not for filthy lucre, but of a ready mind ; neither as being lords over God's heritage, but being examples of the flock. And when the *Chief Shepherd* shall appear, ye shall receive a crown of glory that fadeth not away."

Laymen of the Church ! " Now we beseech you, brethren, to know them who labor among you, and are over you in the Lord, and admonish you, and to esteem them very highly in love for their work's sake, and be at peace among yourselves."

CHAPTER V.

Methodism—What are Her Assurances for Future Success ?

WE have referred, in other chapters, to the rapid increase of the Methodist Church in numbers and wealth ; to her present great educational advantages ; to her peculiar polity, organic unity, and great efficiency, and to her dangers and duties. We come now to inquire, *What are her real assurances for future success ?*

These are mainly dependent upon her continued development of *experimental and practical godliness.*

Methodism, at her beginning, could not be satisfied with mere forms and ceremonies in religion, nor in mere assent to the " Thirty-nine Articles" of Faith of the Established Church, nor in the claims of that Church to exclusive divine rights through " apostolic succession." But she sought for *genuine* and *deep* Christian experience, and found it, in spiritual regeneration, divine adoption, and holy communings with God.

She also sought out the *means* of grace by which her Christian graces could *mature* and her flame of devotion be kept *constantly alive* and *on the increase.* She found them in her secret devotions, her scriptural studies, her family altars, her weekly class and prayer meetings, her "love-feasts" and "band meetings ;" in her " spiritual songs," her street-preaching, and her frequent itinerating mission work.

Though poor, despised and persecuted, she has continued thus to go on, under the guiding hand of Providence and by the power of the divine Spirit, from conquest to conquest, and winning her widening way unto this day.

The continued development of experimental and practical godliness will prove her best

SAFEGUARD AGAINST HERETICAL DOCTRINES.

The doctrines of Methodism have been, in all their essentials, unquestioned from the first by all her different organizations, whatever differences have existed in regard to Church polity. This fact may be accounted for mainly from the fact that her doctrines have been tested by human experience. As Christ has said : " If any man shall do my will, he shall know of the doctrine, whether it be of God, or whether I speak of myself." Human depravity, man's guilt and final

accountability, his moral agency, his "justifica-
tion by faith alone," the true divinity of Christ,
his vicarious sacrifice for sin, the witness of the
Holy Spirit to his adoption, and the attainable-
ness of "perfect love," are the essential sentiments of Methodism, and have been tested as
living realities by the personal experience of all
her members who have lived in the sunlight of a
present, free, and full salvation.

If her membership shall earnestly seek to
keep close to Christ, her "all and in all," by a
living faith "a faith, which works by love," she
shall continue, as in the past, "in the unity of
that true faith," which claims him as her "wisdom, sanctification, and redemption." Thus,
building upon "the sure foundation," the "Rock
of Ages," against her the gates of hell cannot
prevail.

Pure love to God and man will have a powerful tendency to give the Church

A SAFE DIRECTION TO ALL HER VAST RESOURCES.

It will do this by awakening and keeping
alive a quenchless love for our fallen race, and
by devising right and "liberal things" for their
mental, social, moral, and spiritual elevation and
eternal salvation. It will aim to turn all her
resources, whether by her members, wealth,

20

educational facilities, or her Church benevolent enterprises, into such channels as shall tend to promote "peace on earth, good-will to men, and glory to God in the highest." Such is the mission of genuine Methodism.

True, experimental, and practical godliness in the membership will secure to her

SAFETY IN THE PRACTICAL WORKING OF HER PECULIAR CHURCH POLITY.

That there is great power vested in her own regularly appointed officers for the practical workings of the system none will wish to deny ; but it is a perfectly safe power when all its parts are in good working order. When this whole machinery—not of "the great iron wheel," as it has been most unjustly called by some, but more like Ezekiel's vision, of a "wheel within a wheel," moved by "living creatures" under divine direction—is employed for the glory of God and the welfare of mankind, it moves forward without unhealthy friction or serious embarrassments ; but if Methodism shall ever lose her sincere love for Christ's holy cause (the only element in which her ecclesiastical organism or that of any other Church can be safely worked) she will find that severe strains and ruptures will follow. Her real safety can be found only in the constant development of deep Christian experience and its practical outward manifestations. So also will true godliness give the Methodist Church

GREAT CATHOLICITY OF SPIRIT

toward all of every name who love our Lord Jesus Christ in sincerity.

Different denominations of Christians may be likened to the different tribes of Israel on their way to their earthly Canaan—their land of promise. They bore different names, but were under the same leader, were guided by the same " cloudy pillar," ate of the same " manna," drank of the same " rock," and were bound to the same Canaan.

An enlightened Christian charity will extend the hand of fellowship to all who belong to God's modern spiritual Israel, and bid them God-speed in " every good word and work."

Sectarian bigotry cannot live in a truly devoted heart. Christians, from their different stand-points of observation, see things differently, as do those who look at mountain scenery. But the more steadily they fix their eyes of faith upon Christ, their blissful center, and the nearer they come to him, the more they shall all " see him as he is." Thus coming so near to each other, all their hearts shall beat in unison, and in blissful harmony shall they together sing,

> " Blest be the tie that binds
> Our hearts in Christian love ;
> The fellowship of kindred minds
> Is like to that above."

Sectarian bigotry is no part of genuine Methodism. It has no right in her ranks, nor will it ever have *place* there if her members live up to her cardinal principles of " loving God with all the heart, and their neighbors as themselves."

This " pure and undefiled religion " in the hearts and lives of the membership of the Church will

SECURE TO HER DIVINE PROTECTION

> " From all assaults of hell and sin ;
> From foes without and foes within."

" The Lord will be round about her, like a wall of fire, and a glory in her midst." No weapon formed against her shall prosper, for the Lord will be her " sun and shield. He will give grace and glory, and no good thing will he withhold from them that walk uprightly."

This pure and experimental godliness will also secure to Christ's Church

THE PRESENCE AND POWER OF HIS HOLY SPIRIT.

This is the rich legacy which Christ has left for his people, which he has promised to "shed on them abundantly," and "to work with them mightily."

What a marvelous power is this for both ministers and members—the presence and power of the Almighty Spirit to indite our prayers, to quicken our hearts, to kindle the flame of devotion on our altars, to work with and for his own servants, as they proclaim the great salvation to their fellow-men, "confirming the word with signs following !"

May "the Lord God of our fathers" be with the Methodist Church ; be with all evangelical Churches ; and "make them a thousand times as many more as they are, and bless them as he has promised to do !"

THE END.

𝔅𝔬𝔬𝔨𝔰 𝔣𝔬𝔯 𝔱𝔥𝔢 𝔉𝔞𝔪𝔦𝔩𝔶,

PUBLISHED BY NELSON & PHILLIPS,

805 Broadway, N. Y.

———◆◆◆———

BIOGRAPHY.

Abbott, Rev. Benjamin,
· Life of. By JOHN FFIRTH. 18mo.................. $0 55

Anecdotes of the Wesleys.
By Rev. J. B. WAKELEY. Large 16mo.............. 1 25

Asbury and his Coadjutors.
By WILLIAM C. LARRABEE. 2 vols................. 2 25

Asbury, Francis,
Life and Times of; or, The Pioneer Bishop. By W. P. STRICKLAND, D.D. 12mo...................... 1 75

Bangs, Rev. Dr. Nathan,
Life and Times of. By Rev. ABEL STEVENS, LL.D.. 1 75
Half morocco 2 25

Biographical Sketches of Methodist Ministers.
By JOHN M'CLINTOCK, D.D. 8vo. Imitation morocco. 5 00

Boehm's Reminiscences,
Historical and Biographical. 12mo................ 1 75

Bramwell, William,
Life of. 18mo..................................... 0 60

Cartwright, Peter,
Autobiography of. Edited by W. P. STRICKLAND, D.D. 12mo. 1 75

Carvosso,
Life of. 18mo.................................... 0 75

Celebrated Women,

Biographies of. With twenty-eight splendid Engravings on steel, executed by the best American artists. Imperial 8vo. Printed on beautifully tinted paper. Turkey morocco, gilt edge and beveled boards $20 00

Chalmers, Thomas,

A Biographical Study. By Jas. Dodds. Large 16mo. 1 50

Christianity Tested by Eminent Men,

Being Brief Sketches of Christian Biography. By Merritt Caldwell, A.M. 16mo.................. 0 60

Clarke, Dr. A.,

Life of. 12mo...................................... 1 50

Clarke, Dr. Adam,

Life of. New. By J. W. Etheridge, M.A. 12mo.. 1 75
Half Calf 2 25

Clark, Rev. John,

Life of. By Rev. B. M. Hall. 12mo....... .... 1 25

Cromwell, Oliver,

Life of. By Charles Adams, D.D. 16mo.......... 1 25

Dan Young,

Autobiography of. By W. P. Strickland, D.D. 12mo. 1 75

Early Crowned.

A Memoir of Mary E. North. 16mo................ 1 25

Emory, Bishop,

Life of. By R. Emory. 8vo...................... 1 75

Episcopius,

Life of. By Frederic Calder. 12mo............. 1 20

Fletcher, John,

Life of. By Rev. Joseph Benson. 12mo........... 1 25

Fletcher, Mrs. Mary,

Life of. By Rev. H. Moore. 12mo................ 1 50

Garrettson, Rev. Freeborn,

Life of. By N. Bangs, D.D. 12mo................ 1 00

www.ingramcontent.com/pod-product-compliance
Lightning Source LLC
Chambersburg PA
CBHW031359270326
41929CB00010BA/1248